Self-Esteem and Early Learning

Second edition

Rosemary Roberts

P·C·P
Paul Chapman
Publishing

For Matthew, Zillah, Ben and Kate

First published 2002, Reprinted 2003.

Paul Chapman Publishing
A SAGE Publications Company
6 Bonhill Street
London EC2A 4PU

SAGE Publications Inc
2455 Teller Road
Thousand Oaks, California 91320

SAGE Publications India Pvt Ltd
32, M-Block Market
Greater Kailash - I
New Delhi 110 048

British Library Cataloguing in Publication Data

A catalogue record for this book is available from the British Library

ISBN 0 7619 4872 4
ISBN 0 7619 4873 2 (pbk)

Library of Congress catalogue record available

Typeset by Dorwyn Ltd, Rowlands Castle, Hants
Printed and bound by the Cromwell Press, Wilts

Contents

Preface

Rosemary Roberts is an experienced practitioner, well known among policy makers in the early years field. She has been honoured with an OBE for her work. In the updated edition of this book, she has slightly changed the title. Words like 'success' and 'achievement' have come to mean that adults put children under pressure at an early age, to perform adult-set tasks. Although this worrying situation is fast changing, it is important that each book in the Series continues to give the strong, consistent messages that are its central concerns.

Rosemary has framed the book as a story about a family situation, weaving into the story the issues that families will meet. The story shows how each family is different, but also that each family shares with others some aspects of living with young children. The reader meets a variety of situations with the family, and explores these through the character of the teenage girl who lives with them. The author stresses the importance of children being unconditionally accepted, and being allowed to have bad feelings as well as good. She shows how adults can give children the support they need, while setting limits in ways which help children to develop and learn in their widening social network.

Tina Bruce, series editor
October 2001

Acknowledgements

First, I want to thank the two families who welcomed me into their homes week after week for two years; especially 'Lily' and 'Joe' and their mothers. For all the insights and pleasure they gave me, I owe them more than I can say.

I am particularly grateful to Chris Athey, Daphne Briggs and John Howson for all their comments and help, so willingly given.

Above all, my thanks are due to Tina Bruce, whose suggestion it was that I should write this book. Her consistent encouragement, confidence and assistance enabled me to complete it.

Thank you to all the children, families and colleagues with whom I have worked and from whom I have learned so much: in various places, particularly at Elms Road and at PEEP.

Finally a special thank you to my own family and friends; for their interest and support and for all that they have taught me.

Preface for the 0–8 series

The 0–8 Series has stood the test of time, maintaining a central place among early childhood texts. Practitioners have appreciated the books because, while very practical, the Series presents a holistic approach to work with young children, which values close partnership with families and their communities. It is evidence based, drawing on theory and research in an accessible way.

The 0–8 Series, now being revised and updated, continues to deal with the themes of early childhood which have always been of concern and interest to parents, practitioners and the children themselves. The voice of the child has, since 1989, been under threat in education. Each author has made an important contribution in their field of expertise, using this within a sound background of child development and practical experience with children, families, communities, schools and other early childhood settings. The Series consistently gives a central place to the interests and needs of children, emphasising the relationship between child development and the socio-cultural learning with which biological and brain development is inextricably linked. The voice of the child is once again being understood as being important if children are to develop and learn effectively, and if adults helping them to learn (teaching them) are to be effective in their work.

The basic processes of communication, movement, play, self-esteem and understanding of self and others, as well as the symbolic layerings in development (leading to dances, reading, writing, mathematical and musical notations, drawing, model-making) never cease to fascinate those who love and spend time with children. Some of the books in this series focus on these processes of development and learning, by looking at children and their contexts in a general way, giving examples as they go. Other books take a look at particular aspects of individual children and the community. Some emphasise the importance of rich physical and cultural provision and careful consideration of the environment indoors and outdoors and the way that adults work with children.

As Series Editor I am delighted to re-introduce the 0–8 Series to a new readership. The re-launched series enters a more favourable climate than the original series, which survived (and flourished) in a hostile climate of literacy hours for four-year-olds, adult-led learning, and a lack of valuing diversity, multi-lingualism, imagination and creativity. This revised and updated 0–8 Series will inform, support and inspire the next generation of early childhood practitioners in the important work they do, in a climate which will encourage rather than undermine.

I look forward to seeing the impact of the 0–8 Series on the next decade.

Professor Tina Bruce
University of North London
October 2001

Introduction

Parents, and other people who live and work with children, often say they mind about three things. First, that children are happy; second, that they are learning successfully; and third, that they are growing up into caring and responsible adults. This book is about these three things: children's feelings, their learning, and their place in society.

Running like a thread from chapter to chapter is the subject of children's self-concept and the development of their self-esteem. This is seen in this book to be at the heart of how children feel, how they learn and how they relate to other people.

Although the surroundings in which most children grow up have changed greatly in the course of the last century, and ideas of what to do with babies and children keep on changing too, the range of young children's feelings remains the same. We cannot remember many of our own feelings in early childhood; but for all of us, our parents and our children, the emotional map was, and still is, the same.

This book proposes the importance of some of the features of that emotional map in relation to our changing world and what we now know about how children learn. The pride of place given to the personal, social and emotional curriculum in the Curriculum Guidance for the Foundation Stage in England (DfEE 2000) is evidence of a major adjustment in thinking over the previous decade. The book is written for the important people – parents, teachers, nursery nurses and others – who have, or will have, responsibility for children and who therefore, like it or not, have power and influence over them. The themes are common to all families and cultures.

The book's purpose is to use the realisation that 'we've all been there' to manage more successfully and happily the challenge of living with children and their feelings, at home or at work. It suggests that we look for a sense of balance in a range of complicated situations: for instance, understanding the child's point of view as well as our own; accepting the normality of bad feelings as well as good ones; finding ways of accepting feelings at the same time as setting limits for behaviour. Often we need to remember the other side of the coin, rather than being 'admirably single-minded'. Perhaps what is needed is a new virtue for our time: multi-mindedness.

How this book is organised

The book falls into six parts, with two chapters in each part. The first chapter in each part is mainly about the *child's* point of view. These chapters can be read directly in relation to the children with whom we now live and work, but equally they may be relevant to our own early experiences and feelings and the ways in which those now influence our responses to children.

The second chapter in each part focuses more on what it feels like to be the *adult* and on ways in which we can make the most of our opportunities to support the children with whom we live and work.

The chapters consist of story and comment. The story is based on the author's observations of children and their families from various cultural backgrounds, at home and at school. However, none of the characters directly represents any particular individual. Throughout the comment sections are occasional references to the bibliography, intended for those who want to follow up particular points; there is no need to be concerned with them otherwise

Most importantly, each part contains three key statements. In the first chapter of each part these are considered from the child's point of view, and in the second from an adult perspective. These key statements are collected together in the Postscript at the end of each section, with questions and suggestions for further reading.

Prologue

'*My name is Joanne, I live with Mum and the kids, and their dad. Mum isn't my real mum, although I wouldn't mind if she was. The kids' dad isn't my dad either; he knew my real mum when I was a baby and she was very ill. My dad's not around now.*

I came to live with them two years ago, when I was fifteen. Joe was just born then and Lily was two.'

Prologue

PART 1

BABIES FIRST

1

Children learning to be lovable

– INTRODUCING JOE –

❛'What do you want?' Mum often mutters this to herself while she watches one of them with that friendly puzzled look. I like hearing her say that, I think it makes them feel safe. All the time I've been living with Mum and their dad, she's been watching them; not in an interfering way but because she loves them and wants to know about them. That's why they feel so safe. Sometimes I think she watches me a bit too. I hope so.

Once Joe and Lily (she's his sister) were sitting in the big bath upstairs having a great time playing. I love the way Joe looks in the bath. His curls go even tighter; and his skin is lovely and dark like his dad's. Mum was holding the towel and looking at his hair – it always looks like it's a bird's nest at the back these days.

'Joe, what shall we do with your hair?' He stopped playing and looked back at her.

'What shall we do?' she asked again. He filled the little pot he had in his hand with water and lifted it towards his head as if he was going to pour it over his hair.

'Oh no, don't get it all wet as well!,' Mum said hastily. Joe watched her anxiously holding the back of his head with his other hand.

'Mum?' he said, doubtfully. 'Mum?'

'We'd better wash your face,' she said. Joe screwed it up to be ready for the horrible moment, knowing it would make her laugh. When she laughs, he knows she loves him.

The kids' dad was really upset last week. I heard him telling one of his friends how awful it is when your baby doesn't want you. I know Joe does love his dad, and they play lots of games, but Joe had been really miserable. Mum and their dad sometimes call him 'Double Trouble', and that day he was. The others were fed up too; Lily said she wouldn't be so naughty. (Wouldn't she just?) Mum said she's never caught up on sleep since he was born, but he always used to be so good in the daytime that she managed the nights somehow. Mum said she can't keep feeding him all night, but that's what he wants, and now he's being furious and miserable all the time. I saw him really hurt himself the other day when he wanted another biscuit, and Mum said, 'No'. He was in such a rage that he banged his head on the washing machine by mistake and cried and cried.

Today was better; though. Mum and Joe and I were in the kitchen, and Mum was telling me about her friend who is having a new baby. I think Joe thought Mum was smiling at him, and he gave her a great big grin. When she noticed, she stopped talking and grinned back at him. The kitchen was really quiet, and Joe crawled over to where she was standing by the sink. He bent right over and rested his forehead on her feet and he looked so loving and helpless. After that, he looked up at her; and he was still grinning! So Mum picked him up and gave him a big hug. **9**

Babies and young children need to be accepted by their important people

Mothers and other important people

Who are babies' and young children's 'important people'? Of course, parents are important, and so – if there are any – are brothers and sisters; then there are other members of the family, friends and teachers . . . and so the circle gradually widens. But let's start at the beginning – the very beginning. For nine months, the baby has been completely surrounded by the mother, and, although we are only beginning to find out about the baby's life in the womb, there can be no doubt that, when a baby is born, the baby and the mother have already learned things about each other through their bodies that no one else can possibly know. This makes the mother the first 'important person' (Winnicott, 1964, pp. 19–24).

The first important person usually, although by no means always, continues to be the mother. But what about fathers? And what about other carers? Many fathers would say that their baby knew them right from the start. We cannot be sure of the reasons for this, although it is certainly often the case (Brazelton, 1992, p. 35). Whether the answer is to be found in nature or nurture or a combination of both, one thing is clear: a baby must come to know someone before he or she is able to see that person as 'important'. As the mother is the first important person, she acts as the mediator for the baby's subsequent important people, who are, initially, substitutes for her, and who may sooner or later come to be just as important. This often happens with fathers who share much of the childcare and take over the role of the mother in many ways.

Earliest learning

Babies can already do many important things when they are born. They can breathe, digest, protest, respond, interact and, most important of all, they can learn (Gopnik, et al, 1999). They are, however, completely dependent on others for food, warmth and love and they learn naturally in order to survive. In the womb, the rate of learning has been gradual, and the experiences relatively controlled; then, from the moment of birth, the rate of learning suddenly accelerates. Perhaps this accelerated learning is like a hectic toboggan ride. Starting steadily along the brow of the hill, the baby is suddenly pushed onto the steep slope and hurtles down, unable to stop or go back. Gradually adjusting to the breathtaking speed, the baby begins to make some sense of the surroundings as they flash by and starts to realise the possibilities of steering the toboggan.

In that first headlong plunge of the first year, the baby needs to feel safe, with some sense of being held and the knowledge that someone is there to steer for the time being. Within the womb, there was never, of course, any question about someone being there; but at birth, just when the landscape changes dramatically and the baby needs 'holding' most urgently, the mother becomes much less reliable. in fact, now that she is not attached, she sometimes even goes away. The baby needs food, warmth and love, and reassurance that he or she will not be abandoned (Selleck and Purves, 1999).

Unconditional acceptance

Before birth, a baby is 'contained' – physically – by the mother; it is this containment that keeps the baby safe, so that he or she can grow. After birth, although that containment can never again be so absolute, the baby's mother and other important people continue to provide substitutes for it. It is reflected in the mother's physical care and also in the way in which she 'holds' the baby in her mind, accepting the baby's developing personality without judgment. For the baby, the mother's physical care is also a psychological matter (Leach, 1997, pp. 142–4, and Winnicott, 1964, p. 183). Just as they are physically dependent, so babies and young children also need to have their feelings contained by their important adults until they themselves have learned how to manage them. In this way, they are doubly dependent; learning to be acceptable is important, for physical and psychological survival.

The sort of acceptance that babies and young children need from parents and other important people is acceptance that is independent of their behaviour; it is acceptance *of the child* without reservations and without judgments. Forty years ago Carl Rogers described it as 'unconditional positive regard' (Rogers, 1961, p. 62). This is not to say that a parent or carer must suspend all judgments about the actions of the baby or child in question; it is simply that a parent or carer's *unconditional* acceptance *of the child himself* is not threatened by these judgements.

Babies learn that they are acceptable by experiencing, day by day, the results of that acceptance. Every time the father smiles at the baby, every time the mother is there when needed, the baby knows more certainly that he or she is accepted. And when the mother is not there, the baby is not so sure. Some babies take this uncertainty very calmly, while some find it intolerable. Every baby is temperamentally unique, with different responses to the whole range of emotions experienced in all cultures and places.

This kind of acceptance is important for all babies and young children and the bedrock of confidence that can develop as a result is especially crucial for those children who have a growing awareness that they are different from others. This may be because of an impairment, or because they happen to be in a minority in some way.

It is inevitable that sometimes a baby or young child will feel abandoned, and the sense of being acceptable and cared for will be threatened. Since being cared for is essential for a baby's continued existence, the baby learns about how to avoid losing the carer (Miller, 1979, p. 22). When an 'important person' smiles at the baby, and when that person comes at the baby's call, the sense that he or she is acceptable is confirmed. This is not simply a passive process; all the time the baby is learning by experience how to win the smiles, how to bring the person. Every experience is a learning experience.

– JOE'S JOKES –

❝Joe made us laugh the other day. I love the way he's such fun to play with; anything we do, he does it too – well, almost anything. Lily was sitting on the sofa watching the telly and trying to balance him on her lap. Her lap's not quite big enough, and he was a bit wobbly but he was all right really. Anyway when Mum came near, he made this 'I'm not really safe' whimpering sort of noise and put on a pathetic face. When Mum saw it, she couldn't help laughing, and nor could I. When he saw us thinking he was funny he knew it was a joke and laughed as well. It's like when he sees you smiling at him, he always smiles back.

The way Joe thinks he's a clown and makes us laugh makes me wonder about that time when he just wouldn't eat. He was born in September; and this was round about February or March. Mum kept saying it was time to start that mushy stuff babies have, but she didn't really want to, it was everyone else saying it really. He was quite happy just with her feeding him, too. Anyway one day she decided she'd better give it a go, so she mixed some up, and he opened his mouth, and in it went. Once was enough, though! He looked so disgusted and astonished that Mum laughed but that was one time he didn't laugh too. He screwed up his face and shut his mouth really tight, and if Mum managed to get any between his gums he spat it straight out again. One time when she took the spoon away he risked opening his mouth and babbling at her crossly. It sounded exactly like he was saying, 'What are you doing this for? I've told you I hate it, why do you go on?' Quite soon after that, he opened his mouth really wide, but that was only because he got upset about it all and started to cry.

I don't think Mum really wanted him to eat mush then, anyway – she just thought he ought to. Perhaps that's why he wasn't keen either.

Why did I start talking about that? Oh yes, it's the way he thinks. He thinks he's a clown, so he makes us laugh, and he thinks he's a baby so he drinks milk from Mum. He doesn't think he's big, like Dan across the road – at least, not yet – so he doesn't *go to school and he doesn't think he's big like Lily – at least, not yet – so he doesn't eat things with a spoon. It all depends what he thinks.*

I know what he does think though. He thinks he can talk. Ever since the day Joe popped out, Mum's been having conversations with him. She does it all the time. When he was only a few weeks old, I saw her having one of those chats with him that you have with babies. I remember thinking that if I'd wanted to make a film, I could have dubbed it and had him saying things so easily – the tone of voice and gestures were there, it only needed the actual words. Mum likes him to tell her things, that's why. She wants him to talk, she shows him how, she knows he will one day and he knows it too.

That was more than a year ago. He doesn't have any problems with eating now. Last week Lily had her friends to tea, and they're all gannets, Mum says, although she does like it when everything gets eaten. When she said, 'Who wants some more?' Joe waved his hand in the air and shouted, 'Me!' louder than any of the others. He ate it all too. I noticed he was watching Lily really carefully and when someone asked her a question and she nodded her head, Joe nodded his too, in exactly the same way. They love it when he copies them. He thinks he's one of them now. **9**

How babies and young children learn to see themselves is significantly affected by their growing knowledge of how to be acceptable to us

Development of self-concept

'You're the best', children might say one day, with conviction; or, on another day, 'You're nasty', with even more conviction. None of us are immune from these judgments, and each one that comes our way is like another feature added to our internal picture of who we are. By the time we are adult, most of us have grown used to our internal picture, and have found ways of rejecting judgments that don't seem to fit, although sometimes a new one gives us a jolt.

'Dan's mum says you're a better mum than her,' said Lily. 'But I don't think so.'
'Hmm,' said Mum, looking thoughtful. 'I wonder why.'

How do we build up our internal picture of who we are? An idea that occurs consistently in the discussion is that we learn about ourselves from other people and events. Particular reference has been made to the roles of 'important' people, especially parents and teachers, in the development of children's self-concept (Dowling, 2000 and Honess and Yardley, 1987).

Observation tells us that babies and young children experience a bewildering and often overwhelming range of emotions that they cannot understand or control. The mother and other important people can play an important part in seeing and understanding the infant as a whole person at a time when the infant's powerful sensations, feelings, excitements and furies act in a fragmenting way, splitting the infant's dawning self-perception (Klein, 1975a, pp. 190–2). If people respond so that the infant comes to feel wholly recognised and accepted, then the infant can recognise and accept himself or herself as a whole person.

The mother's face and body are like a mirror to the baby. In this very early mirroring process, both know that they are accepted by the other. The mother's acceptance forms the basis of the baby's self-concept, and the mother's responses are the first 'brush strokes' for the developing picture.

Body Language

A mother cannot pretend this early acceptance, because her baby knows her intimately in a physical way, and a mother's body language will give her away every time. A baby knows about a mother, not only by how she looks, but by how she sounds, how her body feels, maybe even by smell and taste (Gopnik et al, pp. 27–8). If, as sometimes happens, a mother's feelings for her baby are very mixed at this stage, it is not the end of the world. It helps if the mother can accept these mixed feelings in herself and not struggle against them; the baby or young child may need particular understanding and very explicit unconditional acceptance later on.

So babies learn about being acceptable with their first language: that is, not by the speech that we usually mean when we refer to language, but by body language. Babies develop this way of learning and communicating in order to survive, needing it long before they know the commonly accepted meanings of spoken words. They use body language before birth and, once this way of communicating is established, they go on using it, long after they know how to understand and use spoken language. For a while, children revert to using their original way of knowing whether they are acceptable to check what people say. At first, particularly because they tend to accept the literal meanings of what we say, they often find that spoken and body language are not consistent. This can be very confusing and upsetting for them (Donaldson, 1978 and Harris, 1989).

'Why doesn't Dan's mummy ever smile at me when I go over there?' asked Lily. 'She said I was always welcome to go and play with Dan, but I don't think she really wants me.'

In adulthood, and across cultures, we vary enormously in the extent to which we retain our original language – body language – for understanding and communicating feelings. Some people continue to rely on this to a large extent, some use both sorts of language, sometimes comparing the different sets of 'evidence', and others abandon the roots of their self-knowledge and put their faith in the spoken word. In the same way that we vary in how we receive communications about ourselves, we also vary in our conscious awareness of both what we actually feel and the messages we give about our feelings (Claxton 1997 and Rogers, 1961, pp. 338–46).

Babies need genuine acceptance – mothers and other important people cannot pretend. There is a very early balancing act in the interaction between the mother and baby: as the mother consciously and unconsciously shows the baby what she recognises and accepts, the baby learns to *be* the sort of person she will recognise and accept. If she is able to recognise and accept *all* the baby's feelings as important, then the baby will be able to recognise and accept them also. The baby's developing self-perception reflects that he or she is growing into a whole person who has a mixture of feelings. Initially, a mother may accept, and thus hold, some feelings for the baby until they are manageable. Then there will come a time when, because the baby *can* accept feelings of pain, anxiety and anger as genuine and legitimate, he or she can begin to learn to deal with them.

We often talk, though, of babies as being good, lovable, awful, or difficult. All the time, and unavoidably, we give babies and young children signals about what we love in them, what we approve of and how we want them to be. It is a natural way of showing them how to be acceptable, both to us and to the world in general. The child's developing self-perception is inextricably linked with learning to be acceptable; but being acceptable sometimes means not showing pain, fear or anger. So it happens that some children learn to exclude pain, fear and anger from their perceptions of themselves: unable either to control those feelings or have them safely accepted by someone else, they manage to 'lose' them in order to be acceptable (Winnicott, 1986, pp. 65–70).

We know about losing things from the work of Piaget (1953, p. 211). Just because you can't see something, that doesn't mean it has ceased to exist (see Chapter 2).

– INTRODUCING LILY –

❝ *Mum's done the same trick with Lily as with Joe. Lily thinks she can read. I was watching her the other day sitting on the floor with her back against the sofa. The floor was covered with bits of jigsaw, heaps of books, her dolls, Joe's Duplo and lots of those old conkers and fir cones from last autumn, all mixed up together. Joe was off with Mum in the kitchen, hoping for another biscuit. Lily had the Nursery Rhymes book on her lap and she was kind of leafing through it like Mum does when she's looking for a good one to sing. Sometimes Lily sang one all the way through and she* nearly always got it right. She put her finger on the words, too – not the right ones, though!

When she came to the end, she dropped it on the floor and picked the next one up off the pile, which was the one with the holes in it, about different animals. Not the caterpillar one – the one with a goat and a monkey. You're supposed to look through the holes as though the book was a mask and pretend to be that animal. When she did it, she got that far-away look, when you know she's thinking about something else completely. When she got to the lion, she started making fierce roaring noises, and thought she was going to tear us all to bits. Luckily it was a baby rabbit on the next page!

It reminded me of when she came home from playgroup pretending to be the grown-up. It was so clever of her; pretending to be someone else. She was really fed up with Joe because Mum's still feeding him. I reckon she thinks he's had Mum quite long enough, especially now Joe does more things like her – if she hasn't got Mum any more like that, why should Joe have her? Anyway she pretended to be the grown-up so that she could make Joe have the dummy that Dan's baby left behind. She knew that, as Lily she couldn't make Joe take the dummy. But as a grown-up – well, grown-ups can make anyone do anything, can't they? When Mum asked her to only pretend with the dummy and not do it for real, Lily just hit Joe. I suppose she couldn't think of another way to put him in his place – where she wants him, instead of where he is.

A couple of weeks ago, Mum had to go away for a few days. The kids' dad looked after them, and they had a great time. Lily's really funny now, though – she keeps acting like she's Mum. The first time she did it was when she came down and found me just taking my coat off. She put on this deep voice she uses to be grown-up and asked me if I would prefer tea or coffee! It made me feel really special, to think that she thought of asking all by herself. Then she took Joe outside into the garden and let him play with her dolls. She said they were off to visit the jungle, and when I asked what the jungle would be like, she put on the deep voice and said, 'It's got toys and dinosaurs in it'. Then she gave me a secret, laughing sort of look and added, 'and flying beds in the sky.'

The next day Mum came back, and Dan's mum came over with Dan and their baby. Dan's baby is too small to play with Joe, but Dan and Lily play a lot. Mum had to go out, so Dan's mum was keeping an eye on things – at least, that's how she saw it. Now that Lily knows how to be 'Mum', though, she thinks she can be in charge. She did help Dan's mum, but I think she thought Dan's mum was helping her. Dan needed a blanket for his game, and Lily explained that they only had duvets now, but she said he could have a cushion if he liked. But when Dan's mum wanted to change Dan's trousers, she forgot about being Mum and ran off so that he would follow. Dan's mum was cross and said would they please come back and stop being so naughty. When Dan looked as though he might be going to wee on the carpet, Lily put on the deep voice and offered to run and fetch the potty. She was just in time, too!⁹

Babies and young children generally behave according to how they see themselves

Behaving in character

On the whole, people behave 'in character'. In other words, what we do makes sense in terms of how we see ourselves (Curry and Johnson, 1990, pp. 27–8). When a person does something that seems 'out of character', the reason may be that the person sees himself or herself differently from the way the rest of us do. Our knowledge and perception of other people is based on the evidence of what they do, what they say and how they look. Our self-concept is based on evidence, too, but how we see this is affected by the mirror process of how others see us. It is also affected by our ideas of what we *could* do if we chose – what we can imagine ourselves doing.

This works the other way around as well. We tend not to do things we do not think of ourselves as doing. 'I wouldn't dream of doing such a thing,' you might say, or, 'Nothing was further from my mind'. Although people sometimes surprise themselves by what they do, it is worth remembering that our minds work on a subconscious level for much of the time, and that subconscious wishes and needs can be even more powerful than conscious ones.

Self-concept in relation to behaviour

The idea that we tend to behave according to how we see ourselves seems at first rather a limited view. If we need to envisage doing something before we are likely to do it, how can we learn to behave in new ways? Of course, you only have to do something once, such as catching a ball or making someone laugh, to get the idea that you are now a person who catches balls and makes people laugh, and then you can do these things anytime (Erikson, 1950, p. 211). Sometimes this happens by chance, but often someone else says something like, 'Why don't you have a go, I know you can do it'. A possibility in someone else's mind suddenly becomes a possibility in our own. As Joanne said about Joe:

> *He thinks he's a clown so he makes us laugh . . . it all depends what he thinks.*

One important way that children learn to behave in new ways is in pretend play. By pretending to be someone else, they can behave like that person (Light, 1979, pp. 41–61). The rules are strict:

> *'I am Mum today, so I can only do what Mum would do' or 'I am being the Bad Baby, so I can . . .!'*

In their play, children often adopt characters from favourite television programmes or stories, and this can have a profound influence on their developing sense of self. They 'think themselves into role' as thoroughly as professional actors, but at a time when their own sense of identity is still in the making.

This 'trying on' of personality (remember we actually refer to children 'trying it on') is a wonderful, natural, safe way of exploring how to be acceptable – of rummaging about in the possibilities. Children 'try it on' with their important adults, as they do with each other. It is a way of trying out how to behave, without committing themselves; they are completely in control, ending the experiment at any moment by dropping the role. It also enables them to explore their reactions to painful and frightening situations – for instance violence or death – at the safer distance of one remove from reality. Children who have been able to do this are better able to manage those situations in real life.

How children see themselves and how they behave as a result of their self-perception are such complex and interrelated aspects of self that it is helpful to find a way of untangling the threads and considering them one at a time. Then it becomes possible to get an idea of what is happening to these threads in individual children. Curry and Johnson (1990, pp. 5–9) suggest using four areas: acceptance, power and control, moral worth and competence.

Between child and mother, between child and other important people, between brothers and sisters and between friends, the factor of acceptance is at the heart of self-concept. Infants and young children are starting on the struggle for the second factor, power and control. This is not only about exerting control over their environment; it is also about achieving self-control. The third area, moral worth, refers to the child's developing concept of good and bad, right and wrong. The fourth area, competence, relates to the child's developing social, emotional, physical and cognitive skills, his or her ability to solve problems and the resulting sense of competence.

Much of the most influential work on the very early development of self-concept was carried out between 1950 and 1980. Although there has been a great deal of research and writing in relation to the brain and to the development of curricula, the earlier work on self-concept remains important today. It still appears that the development of behaviour and the development of self-concept are inter-dependent, and that in thinking about the development of one, we also need to think about the development of the other. Self-concept profoundly influences behaviour everywhere – in families, in schools, in our world.

2

Being important adults

– DAD'S HOME! –

' 'We're home,' called Mum as she came through the door. She'd left Joe in his push-chair while she went into the kitchen to put the kettle on. Lily trailed in after her, holding Christina (that's her doll) by one leg, and looking hot and tired. It was Saturday and we'd been at the park nearly all afternoon. Lily always goes to the swings first, and now Mum pushes her really high, so the chains go slack at the top and the world stands still. She loves that. I never see her walk in the park, she always has to run, all the time.

Mum went to get Joe out of his chair; and Lily took Christina into the back room. And guess what? There was her dad! He'd come home early and was sitting so quietly that we didn't know he was there. He didn't say a word, and nor did Lily – she just stood right in front of him and grinned at him, and he grinned back at her. I thought I'd be pretty happy if anyone was that pleased to see me!

'Hello, Tiger Lily!' He often calls her that, because of her bubbly gold hair; and because he says she's fierce. Once they were looking at themselves together in the bathroom mirror; with dad's black face and Lily's gold one.

'Definitely a tiger lily,' he said to her; grinning and tickling her to make her laugh.

'Been to the park?' he asked. 'What did you play on?' She told him all about the swing and about the girl who wouldn't go home when her brother told her to. (Though she didn't tell him that she wouldn't either, when Mum said.) Then he wanted to know about the rest of her day and what she had for lunch and if she'd enjoyed it. I think Lily's lucky to have him for her dad. He asked her all that stuff to let her know he hadn't forgotten her while he was out, and because he really wanted to know if she'd had a good day. Lots of dads ask because they want to know if you've been good or helpful or learned a lot. Then if you haven't, they don't want to know any more. '

Babies and young children need to be accepted by their important people

Holding

From the very earliest days, babies begin to build up their own internal ability to deal with their feelings. This ability is based on a growing feeling of internal strength, or wholeness, and a child's consciousness of being known and accepted is what helps that ability to grow (Bettelheim, 1987, pp. 146–65). Feelings of internal wholeness, and of disintegration, are reflected in the language we use to describe them. 'She's a "very together" person,' we might say, or 'I'm falling to pieces'.

Babies' actions often reflect their efforts to 'hold themselves together'.

Joe held the piece of orange firmly, first in his right hand, then in both. He put it very cautiously into his mouth and hastily removed it again after one tentative lick, screwing up his face as he did so. A second later, he tried again, this time tasting it for longer and screwing up his face less, as though he was getting used to the sharpness and really quite liked it. All this time he was holding it with both hands and looking at it carefully each time he took it out of his mouth. It seemed to make all the difference that he was holding something in both hands that also felt and tasted good in his mouth – as if the piece of orange was holding him together in some way, and without it he would fall apart and be miserable again.

Sometimes the strain of 'holding themselves together' gets too much for babies and young children, and this is when important people can help. When they feel they are falling to pieces, they need a sense of being held, until they can manage again for themselves. There are various ways of giving this sense; it can come from physical action or from mental awareness. Who we are in relation to the child and where we are will dictate which ways are most appropriate. For a four-year-old at bedtime, a cuddle might be most appropriate; for the same four-year-old in the nursery setting, a pretend game inside a big cardboard box might be the answer; sometimes just not being forgotten is what is needed – the child needs to know that he or she is 'held' in the important person's mind.

Knowledge and acceptance

Young children need to feel accepted, but, alongside that acceptance, they need to feel known. In terms of reassurance, acceptance only works if it comes with knowledge, and knowledge only works if it comes with acceptance.

If we are accepted by someone who doesn't know us very well, we fear that once that person 'knows the worst', their acceptance may turn to rejection. If acceptance is to work as the basis of positive self-concept, it must be based on knowledge. On the other hand, it is not reassuring to be well known by someone when their acceptance is in doubt; to be rejected, at any stage in life, by an important person who knows us well is indeed devastating. This is why being known but not necessarily accepted feels so precarious.

Rejection is a kind of loss, and, right from day one, babies and young children experience other losses which are a normal part of life. They lose the safety of the womb, the comfort of the breast, the presence of important people: day after day, life is made up of a series of little losses, together with occasional major ones. This is not to say that life is miserable for babies; fortunately, they live very much 'in the present', and of course they gain things as well as losing them. But from the ego-centric viewpoint of the baby or young child, each loss represents a rejection. These rejections must be balanced by acceptance if the baby is to grow up feeling acceptable.

At the stage when children start to belong to groups outside the family, such as a childcare group or school setting, possible rejection takes on new meaning. It has been shown that children remember experiences of rejection by their peers and teachers with painful clarity (Gussin Paley, 1992, pp. 33–6). It can be argued that our job as important adults in these settings should include efforts to guard against 'the habit of rejection', whatever its cause. For physical, temperamental or biographical reasons, some children seem to be particularly precarious in this respect; they need to know that they are acceptable in order to learn.

Power of important adults

It is the possibility of knowledge without acceptance, or acceptance without knowledge, that gives us such power over the children for whom we are responsible. Because we are 'important', it is possible for us to devastate children by withholding or withdrawing our acceptance. The closer we are to children, and the better we know them, the more powerful we become.

There is, however, the other side of this coin. As our knowledge of a child gradually grows, our acceptance of that child carries more and more conviction. Important people may have the power to devastate by rejection, but they have the corresponding power to support and build through their acceptance.

A doctor's success in helping a child to be well or a teacher's success in helping a child to learn – or, of course, a parent's success in doing both – is directly related to his or her knowledge about the child. Success is thought to depend on a good 'match', of medical treatment to the growing body or of learning experiences to the developing mind. It can be argued that there is another, completely different but equally significant reason for gaining as detailed a knowledge of a child as possible. This reason is related to the child's self-concept. We tend to use the knowledge of children which we have gained by being 'important people' to look after them and help them to learn. We may, in addition, offer it back to the child in the form of realistic acceptance. The greater the depth of knowledge, the greater will be the power of our acceptance. The injunction to 'know the child' can take on a deeper meaning.

– MUM AND JOE –

❛ Sometimes I wonder why Mum loves Joe like she does. If he woke me up like that all night, I reckon I'd feel more like giving him away.

Mum was playing a game with him the other day giving him little bits of bread-stick because he's dribbly and grumpy with his teeth. Then she remembered the chips were cooking, and when she started to go away and look at them, Joe really wailed. She's so tired I thought she'd be cross or take no notice, but she didn't. She came straight back, picked him up and gave him a huge hug. She said, 'You're an old softy aren't you?' and hugged him some more and then took him off to look at the chips with her.

I think she doesn't mind him needing her really; maybe she quite likes it. Perhaps that's why he cries every night, when he wakes up in his cot and wants to be in bed with Mum. He thinks he's in the wrong place, and the right place is with Mum. How can he learn to sleep all night without needing her? ❜

How babies and young children learn to see themselves is significantly affected by their growing knowledge of how to be acceptable to us

---

Adult motivation

Babies begin to discover what sort of a person they are right from the first day. As this process of discovery is well under way before our words can be understood, babies develop other ways of understanding about what matters to their important people; they use their senses to gauge adult and sibling reactions. In our role as important adults, we cannot hide behind words. How we really feel and what we really think are the things with which babies are actually dealing.

If we accept that babies and young children are responding to what we really feel and think, we may feel the need to take an honest look at what we actually *do* mind about. This is probably easier said than done. Often feelings get lost, particularly if they are painful. However, feelings that have become subconscious still affect our reactions to things. Some parents, for instance, find it very difficult to have to listen to their baby crying; others may tolerate crying without feeling deeply upset, but, in spite of 'normal' development, are very anxious about whether the baby is feeding properly. Maybe these reactions are the results of parents' own early childhood experiences; our reactions may alter as we gain experience. In such situations, the responses the baby receives are likely to be governed by our own feelings, needs and priorities.

Parents who need their children to behave in certain ways may be responding to their own childhood. Those who did not experience an atmosphere of acceptance and tolerance as children were deprived; and they may continue, throughout their lives, to need and to seek the unconditional acceptance that their own parents did not give them at the time. In the balance of the generations, important people are in some ways mutual; the parents are important people for the child, but the child is also important for the adult.

So it can happen that, instead of receiving much needed unconditional acceptance, the baby's role is to recognise and accept the needs of one or both parents. As the parents' care is essential for the baby's existence, the baby begins to learn from the first day how to fit in with what the parents need. For example, a young child may learn to accept the food his parent gives him, not because he likes or needs it but because – probably unconsciously – he knows that the person on whom he depends for survival actually *needs* his acceptance in this way. It is 'safer' to eat up than to reject.

Unconscious messages

Some people may recognise their own childhood pattern in this description and may wonder if this means that the pattern inevitably repeats itself. The first step to take in answering this question is to try to do some 'self-watching', and notice the things that do seem, unaccountably or disproportionately, to matter very much. Then it becomes possible to think and talk about those things and to balance them with what we know about the unconditional acceptance that babies and young children need.

Even as we extend unconditional acceptance to babies and young children, they are still learning all the time about how we want them to behave, at different times and in a variety of places. In the author's study of the development of positive self-concept and learning skills (Roberts, 1993), one of the issues to emerge was connected with how parents *feel* about their children's behaviour. The parents' reactions were found to vary, depending on whether the setting was the home or somewhere outside it. At home, positive reactions related to personal characteristics, such as affection, helpfulness and happiness. When out in public, parents were unanimous in their feeling that what matters most of all is that children's behaviour should be 'socially acceptable'. There was a difference, in the parents' view, between ideally acceptable 'home' behaviour – affectionate, helpful and happy – and ideally acceptable 'out' behaviour – conforming, obedient, polite, sociable and sharing.

This raises questions about children's perceptions of appropriate behaviour when they go to school. It must be assumed that, initially at least, school is perceived, by both parents and children, as 'out'. This question will be considered in more detail in Chapter 9. Meanwhile, why should the parents have felt so very strongly about their children's public behaviour?

If we are unsure of our own worth, we have no secure basis for seeing ourselves as acceptable. Those who are unsure about themselves need constant confirmation of their worth. The more important our role as parent or carer is to us, the more we are liable to mind about other people's judgment of our ability in that role.

We tend to be judged, in relation to our ability as parents or carers, by the behaviour of the children in our care. And unless we are very secure in the knowledge of our worth as parents and carers, we need those children to behave in ways that 'do us credit', hence the parents' anxiety about their children's behaviour. However, happiness and the ability to learn – which were the main goals of the parents in the study mentioned above – do not happen as a result of the ability to conform and share, to be obedient, polite and sociable. In fact, early struggles to be socially acceptable are not generally happy experiences, nor are they always consistent with the ways in which successful early learning naturally takes place. Of course it matters that children learn to adapt to the society in which they live, and the child who persistently asks questions and is 'into everything' may in certain circumstances be thought to be behaving badly. But such behaviour is exactly what makes for successful learning. To accept and value and manage it will help the child to see herself as a learner, rather than as naughty.

– LILY'S SUPERMAN –

❝ Dan came to play with Lily yesterday; all dressed up like Superman he was. His mum had lent him her lovely scarf, and it was wound around his shoulders. He marched straight into the hall and announced, 'I'm Superman,' to no one in particular. Then he went up to Lily gave her a great big shove and said, 'Lily' very fiercely right in her face. Lily looked indignant and went straight off to Mum to complain, but she had just opened her mouth and taken a breath when she stopped. She stood there in front of Mum, thinking for a moment, and Mum looked at her and waited. Then she surprised us all by saying very firmly 'Dan's here to play'. And off they went to the kitchen!

It's a good thing Mum doesn't mind a bit of chaos. Lily and Dan spent the rest of the morning playing 'Superman and Superwoman'. They made a house under the table with cushions and bowls and an old blanket, and Lily's dolls had to be the babies. Joe wanted to be in the game too, but he didn't stay long because Lily and Dan were so bossy. They said he was one of the babies, and that he had to be in a baby's place and stay there, so after a while he got fed up and went off to look for

Mum. When Lily and Dan wanted it to be dinner-time, Mum said they'd better have Super-Dinner and she gave them a packet of Lily's favourite Crunchies to share. In the end though Lily got fed up too. She said Dan wouldn't let her share out the Crunchies, and he kept pushing her around. Dan said Superman was supposed to be the boss, and then Mum stopped them arguing by saying that if they didn't come quickly it would be too late to go to the park for a picnic.

Babies and young children generally behave according to how they see themselves

Imaginative play

By their first birthday, babies are already showing signs of self-awareness in the form of imitative play in which they might pretend to drink from an empty cup or comfort a teddy bear (Curry and Johnson, 1990, p. 27). As they grow older, pretend play becomes increasingly important to them (Light, 1979, p. 41). Supporting children's imaginative play is crucial (Bruce, 1996). It is only by pretending to be another person that a child can explore what it would be like to be that sort of person, and this is what children need to do in order to make real choices about themselves in relation to other people. A child who is only ever allowed to be him– or herself cannot begin to understand what it would be like to be another person. This is the gift that drama gives us, and children's pretend play is drama in a very real sense.

Babies and young children have an amazing capacity for observing and remembering. What Dad said to the dog, where Mum left the keys, how the builder smooths cement with a trowel and where you hid the special biscuits – these are all commonplace observations to children, along with details of gesture and intonation. Crucially important role models for pretend play come first and foremost from within the family: mummies and daddies, the baby, even the dog. Children will play these pretend games with 'modern dress' and a bare stage, if costumes and scenery are not available; but when we provide old castoffs for dressing-up clothes, and a few props, this not only adds another dimension to the play, but signals our acceptance and recognition of its importance.

As children's lives unfold and widen to include people and places outside the home, television programmes and stories in books, so their choice of role models for their pretend play widens too. The richer the variety and complexity of characters they have to choose from, the more they will benefit from this sort of play. Allowing and encouraging children's play gives them a safe way to explore and begin to understand themselves, the people in their world and the situations in which they find themselves.

POSTSCRIPT TO PART 1: BABIES FIRST

Living or working with young children? Questions to think about . . .

Babies and young children need to feel accepted by their important people

1. What are some of the things that parents and carers can do to make sure that a baby or young child feels accepted?

How babies and young children learn to see themselves is significantly affected by their growing knowledge of how to be acceptable to us

2. What characteristics and behaviours do you find particularly acceptable in young children? What is unacceptable to you? Why?

Babies and young children generally behave according to how they see themselves

3. Try watching a child very carefully, for about half an hour. What have you learned about that child's self-concept?

RECOMMENDED FURTHER READING

For sharing with children . . .

Waddell, M. & Benson, P. (1992), *Owl Babies*, London, Walker Books
'Once there were three baby owls: Sarah and Percy and Bill. They lived in a hole in the trunk of a tree with their Owl Mother'. This beautiful picture book is always a hit with small children, because they completely understand the plot. It's night-time, and Mum is out. Will she come back?

For a good read . . .

Gopnik, A. et al (1999), *How Babies Think*, London, Phoenix
This fascinating book is about what babies know, and how they learn it. It is a summary of twenty-five years of research in philosophy, psychology, neuro-science and linguistics into the minds of children. 'Parents who read this book should find themselves feeling both the shock of recognition and the shock of the new . . . science and childhood belong together. Everyone should be interested in understanding children because the future of the world, quite literally, depends on them.'

For reference . . .

Leach, P. (1997), *Your Baby and Child*, London, Penguin Books
If you are looking for a thoroughly up to date and reliable guide to childcare and development from a parent or carer perspective, this is it. Based on the latest research and thinking on child development and learning, Penelope Leach's wisdom and common sense are evident in every line of information and advice. And the many photographs are really lovely.

PART 2

FUNDAMENTAL FEELINGS

3

Children's normal bad feelings

– CATS AND DUSTPANS –

❝ I'm the lucky one just now. Lily likes me. I sat down on the floor to play with her the other day and straight away Toby (he's the cat) got on my lap and curled up so I couldn't move. Mum was there too, so she knelt on the floor and sat Lily on her lap, just opposite. Lily gazed and gazed at me so solemnly but when she looked at Toby on my lap, I was glad I wasn't him. After a bit, Toby got down and padded off past where Mum and Lily were, and as he went by, Lily grabbed his tail and pulled it really hard, laughing and looking at me! Mum was cross and told her to stop, so she let go with a flourish and went off to get the biscuit tin. When she'd got the lid off and had a good look inside, she came over to me, holding the tin out with a huge smile.

I was quite surprised that she was angry with Toby because he'd been on my knee. Usually it's Joe that makes Lily feel hurt and angry because he's got Mum. I remember when Mum was trying to feed Joe and help Lily with her play-dough all at the same time. Lily kept asking Mum to do things that needed two hands, so that she would have to put Joe down, and Mum kept managing it without stopping Joe's feeding. I felt sorry for Mum, trying to please everybody, and I felt sorry for Lily too, because she was so desperate. In the end Lily gave up trying to empty Joe's mouth of Mum, and stuffed all the play-dough right into her own mouth instead – if you can't beat 'em, join 'em! And when Mum made her spit it out because it's not for eating, she threw it right across the kitchen. Poor old girl. Joe watched it all from the crook of Mum's arm, with that 'I've got the cream' smile.

Still, Joe doesn't have things all his own way. I remember when he crawled all the way from the far end of the sitting-room to play with the dustpan and brush. He had almost made it, when Mum swooped down and removed it to a safe place. Joe was so furious, he put his head down on the floor and really shouted. Two minutes later he wasn't allowed to play with the big pot of nappy cream either; so he shouted all over again. He must have thought we were following him around spoiling his fun on purpose. ❞

> ## As well as feeling love and pleasure, it is normal for babies and young children to feel pain, anxiety and anger

Normal mixed feelings

'Don't worry . . . be happy . . .' goes the song. When a new baby is born, in whatever culture or situation, there are always worries mixed with the happiness, and adjustments to be made. As a baby grows into childhood, our job as important adults may become more and more challenging, sometimes even overwhelming. One of the most difficult things for us to manage is children's expressions of pain, anxiety or anger. If a baby or young child is still unhappy or angry even after we have done our best, we may feel exhausted, rejected – a failure.

When we think of normal 'bad' feelings, it helps to remember the normal 'good' feelings of love and pleasure which also make up our lives with babies and young children. Quite rightly, love and pleasure for children are often our first consideration; but if they are the *only* consideration, we run a risk by ignoring other, more negative, feelings.

Unavoidably, and in the normal course of events, babies and young children have a very great deal in their lives that hurts, that is worrying and that is infuriating. It would not be desirable, even if it were possible, to protect them entirely from these normal real-life experiences, as they represent a crucial source of learning. Consequently, we have to live with babies' and young children's expressions of pain, anxiety and anger. This can be made a great deal easier by understanding as much as possible about what these emotions may feel like for them.

Reasons for 'bad' feelings

What does it feel like for the child whose life is just beginning? To find some answers to this question, we can only study our own 'important children' at home or work, as much and as carefully as possible. We can also learn from the writings of people who have studied other babies and young children.

Some experiences are common to all children. The abrupt emergence into a world after nine months in the womb is both a liberation and a stark shock. At birth, the freedom from the confines of the womb and birth canal is combined with the new effect of the full force of gravity, so that every movement requires both less and more effort than before. Gone are the familiar sights, sounds and sensations of the months before birth; suddenly the world is vast, bright, noisy, smelly and unknown. After the loss of the womb comes a different set of life-lines involving breathing, feeding, people and places. Every experience for the baby contains the possibility of pleasure, the probability of loss: the feed must end, the cuddle will not last forever, the nappy must be changed (Miller, L., 1992a). In small ways, the baby is learning to live with loss day by day. Some babies, on occasion, seem to find this quite overwhelming. A loved person goes out or the room looks different, and their world collapses.

Crying

Babies cry for a variety of reasons. D.W. Winnicott (1964, pp. 58–68) suggests that there are four normal kinds of crying. His first reason was that babies cry in order to feel that they are exercising their lungs. Winnicott suggests that pleasure can enter into crying as it can into any bodily function, and that this sort of crying is for satisfaction. Then there is the cry of pain: as well as indicating present pain, including hunger, this can signal painful memories or fear of pain.

Babies also cry with rage, and this ability to be angry with another person when things are not right is very important. Being in a rage is frightening for babies and young children because they feel destructive and dangerous; they need the experience of an adult who can tolerate that rage and not be badly hurt or destroyed by it. A calm response in the face of a tantrum gives the child confidence and reassurance about the possibility of accepting and managing those feelings. An adult who feels unable to tolerate a tantrum and tries to avoid one at all costs is confirming a child's fear that, in such a state, he or she is indeed destructive and dangerous, and that the damage cannot be mended.

The fourth type of crying that Winnicott outlines is that of grief: what he calls 'a song of sadness'. An infant's ability to cry from grief is as important as crying from rage, but more complex. Winnicott suggests that this sad crying is an early version of the ability to say 'sorry' and 'thank you', and that receiving the acceptance, sympathy and comfort that babies and children need in this state is much more valuable than teaching the words 'sorry' and 'thank you'.

In her book 'Your Baby and Child' (1997, pp. 113–33), in the section 'Crying and comforting', Penelope Leach strongly disagrees with Winnicott's view that babies may cry for bodily satisfaction. She describes a range of situations that may cause babies to cry, with ways to help them. These include hunger, pain, over-stimulation, shock and fear, mis-timing, being undressed, feeling cold, jerks and twitches, lack of physical contact. The whole section is very helpful, for parents and carers who are struggling both with a crying baby, and with their own feelings as they try to manage and alleviate the baby's distress.

Underlying the routines of day-to-day living for most babies and young children is a strong determination to explore, to find out and to gain control. From birth, this 'need to know' is evident in their behaviour (Gopnik et al 1997). They listen and watch, they struggle to touch, to move, to taste – this is how they find out. Often these explorations are immensely satisfying, but the struggle to do all these things is also beset by frustrations, initially because of the limitations of their own physical ability, and later because often what they want is either incomprehensible or unacceptable to the adult who is in control. Frustrations, especially as a result of not being able to explore, are another major source of normal 'bad' feelings.

Brothers and sisters

A final cause for these normal 'bad' feelings can be brothers and sisters. Judy Dunn (1993, pp. 1–14) tells us that there are many variations in different settings and cultures about the ways in which children relate to each other and to adults. It is important not to make generalisations about such a very complex issue. It must also be clear to anyone who watches children in a variety of situations that very many children gain a great deal of love and pleasure from relationships with their brothers and sisters.

At the same time, however, there can be no doubt of the potential for normal 'bad' feelings between siblings. For a young child, the arrival of a new baby means that – however much is to be gained – the child who was the previous 'baby' will no longer enjoy the exclusive relationship that existed with the mother, but must give it up to someone else. This often coincides with weaning, which means losing the mother's breast and/or bottle as the main source of nourishment and cuddles. Of course, there is much to be said for being 'the grown-up one', but even so, the displacement from that special place with the mother can be hard to bear. There is much good advice from Penelope Leach (1997, pp. 422–9) on how an older sibling may be feeling at the birth of a new baby, and how to manage during the weeks around the birth, and for the first few months, in order to help that older child.

The 'built-in' difficulties in sibling relationships are not confined to the older child. In an earlier book (1984, p. 55), Judy Dunn writes of the predicament for the younger child:

> *If you grow up from four to ten years old with someone who knows you intimately, spends a great deal of time with you and relentlessly disparages and criticises you, while himself appearing effortlessly more capable and successful, surely this experience will have a profound effect on your sense of your own value and efficacy, and will affect your behaviour with others outside the home.*

Of course, this is not true for all sisters and brothers, but it indicates the ordinary psychological reactions that can result from normal bad feelings at such close quarters.

– MIXED-UP LILY –

❛ *I think Lily is often fierce with the cat because it's safer than being fierce with people, especially Joe. It isn't only when she's angry with Joe, though. There was that time when their dad went away for a fortnight, and after about ten days, I think she was afraid he wasn't coming back. I suppose it's a long time when you're only that old. That was when she got really quiet and she wouldn't let Mum out of her sight, but she was wild with the cat, pulling his tail and shouting 'Eat!' at him when he was eating already. It's safer to kick the cat, isn't it? They might not love her if she kicks them, especially if she does it to Joe; and that's what she's afraid of.*

Lily's such a mixed-up kid when it comes to Joe. The other day she was playing with the Duplo and she kept sweeping the pieces off the table so that they landed on Joe's head, but the next moment she handed him Old MacDonald, which is one of her favourites. Sometimes she plays like she's two people, one laughing and distracting and finding toys, and the other pushing and squeezing and bumping. I think it's great that she plays with him at all, after everything he's taken over from her. I think she really loves him, and it makes her feel better when she can manage the bad feelings enough to make room for the good ones – then she knows she's a good sister. She doesn't only play with him because she knows Mum will be pleased – sometimes she really wants to play with him as well, and then she feels good. **'**

> **Denied pain, anxiety and anger all undermine positive self-concept – these feelings are hard to acknowledge and manage unless they are recognised by others as normal and acceptable**

Acknowledging 'bad' feelings

We seem to spend a lot of time and energy denying pain, fear and anger and trying to eliminate these emotions from our lives. We may avoid the causes, by not speaking to someone or withdrawing from a situation. Alternatively, we may try to 'pass on' our feelings to someone else, for instance by being irritable with someone who had nothing to do with the reason for our feelings. Often, this person will be someone in whose love we have confidence and with whom it is therefore 'safe' to be irritable. So when things get bad, our inclination is often to keep out of the way or, if we can't do that, to 'dump' our feelings on the nearest 'safe' person.

Babies and young children quickly begin to develop the ability either to avoid pain, fear and anger (requiring some form of anticipation) or to pass on feelings (requiring the ability to communicate, although not necessarily in spoken language). As adults, we tend to encourage this ability: we say things like 'Don't cry', 'Come on, there's no need to be scared', and 'Will you stop making that noise!' Or maybe we use distractions, 'Look, what's your teddy doing on the floor?' and 'Would you like a biscuit?'

However, there are grounds for recognising the great importance, for babies and children, of experiencing their true feelings and coming to know themselves (Miller, A., 1979, pp. 19–29). Children who have not been allowed to express their negative feelings may be in danger of a kind of emotional helplessness. Feelings do not cease to exist simply because they are denied; instead, what tends to happen is that they become all the more powerful for having been ignored. Emotional development is about learning how to accept and manage feelings, both positive and negative, and how to respond appropriately.

Cognitively, evasions and distractions are unhelpful too. Children who have been encouraged to think about something else every time something goes wrong are likely to be low on concentration and persistence in problem-solving situations.

For babies and young children, acceptance of *all* sorts of feelings is possible if they are given enough opportunities to be themselves. However, the need to accept something before it is possible to deal with it – whether the 'something' is an emotion, a person or a situation – must be one of the most unrecognised and unpractised essentials of human relationships. We need to realise that, in order to resolve a situation, we must accept its existence.

Sometimes, however, the unconscious needs of parents prevent children from achieving this acceptance. In the author's study (Roberts, 1993, pp. 67–74), parents were asked about their feelings in relation to their children's behaviour. In answer to the question, 'What does your four-year-old do that makes you feel particularly rejecting and disapproving?', the almost unanimous answer was that forms of verbal protest are the hardest aspect of children's behaviour for their parents to accept. It may be that, in our responses to children, we do accept their feelings, sympathising and trying to resolve the situation; or perhaps we try to refuse to allow the crying, complaints, arguments and quarrels; or maybe we grit our teeth and take no notice. Probably most parents have tried all these, but common-sense and observation would suggest that, when children cry, complain, argue or quarrel, we 'important adults' usually do our best to get them to stop.

We would all like children to learn to deal with their feelings so that there is less crying, complaining, arguing and quarrelling. But that is only possible if children are allowed to *have* the feelings in order to work on them. If we, as 'important adults', feel rejecting and disapproving when children express their negative feelings, the children soon learn to hide them, which makes it impossible to try to accept and resolve them. Hidden feelings are always liable to re-emerge, out of control, as in Black's splendid poem *The Red Judge*. Feelings that have been accepted and thought about are generally more manageable.

The cycle of loss

As discussed in Chapter 1, children need their important people's acceptance; so, if 'bad' feelings are not acceptable, they must be hidden if the child is not to risk losing the most important thing in the world – the acceptance of the important adult.

Miller (1979, pp. 21–3) describes the way in which many adults actually need to be accepted by their children, because of their own parenting. This may be why it is so hard for many of us to tolerate children's protests: when a baby goes on crying in spite of our best efforts, or when a two-year-old has a tantrum, there is a part of us that feels rejected.

Here is what seems to be a frequent cycle of events:

- First, a child feels the need to learn to hide unacceptable 'bad' feelings.
- Second, the child's developing self-perception grows to exclude those hidden feelings.
- Third, the self-concept which has excluded those 'bad' feelings loses them altogether into the subconscious (but losing something does not mean that it ceases to exist).
- Fourth, the growing child is thereby deprived of the opportunity to accept and come to terms with the feelings of pain, fear and anger that are a normal part of early childhood; instead, those feelings remain a dead weight in the subconscious, beyond control.
- Fifth, in adulthood these children may find it hard to manage feelings of pain, anxiety or fear, and anger. They may avoid situations involving those feelings, may consistently need to 'dump' them on others, or may respond very violently. They may also require unconditional acceptance from their own children, because the need for acceptance has not yet been met.

When these things happen, the cycle starts again for the sake of the needy adults. We need to find ways of breaking this repeating pattern, so that our children grow into adults who are better able to understand and manage their own feelings.

– MUM'S MAGIC –

❝ *That time when the kids' dad was away, Lily was struggling to make sense of why he wasn't there. She was really hurting because he was gone. She was confused and sad. I thought Mum did a clever thing to help her: she got out the photos and helped Lily to sort out all the family ones so that she could look at her dad and they could talk about him. After they'd looked at the photos, they talked about what he was doing and when he was coming back, and then he seemed to be real again for Lily. Mum said she missed him, too. Lily was better for a bit after that.*

Mum's really good at understanding when they feel sad because someone's missing. She knows how they feel, even if she can't bring the person back. She's not so understanding when Lily's angry, though; Lily wants to hit people and throw things when she's angry – of course, she mustn't, but even her wanting to do it makes Mum cross. When it's Joe, he just roars, and Mum always wonders what's the matter. She looks at him really carefully, and then he seems to feel safer. She still always tries to stop him roaring though. Can't say I blame her – who wants hitting and throwing and roaring? But it's funny, as soon as she does sympathise they stop anyway; it's when she takes no notice that they go on and on. ❯

Babies and young children can manage pain, anxiety and anger more easily if they know that other people accept and sympathise with how they feel

---

Containment

Most of us have experienced the relief of having someone listen with complete attention while we explain about something that is upsetting us. Even if that person is unable to be of any practical help, the fact that he or she is willing to accept how we feel can be helpful, provided that person is not drawn in to feeling as we do. Calm acceptance by someone else of how we feel helps us to accept and deal with our feelings and to think about appropriate responses; whereas, for instance, panic-stricken or angry acceptance tends to 'stoke up' our own fear or anger. The same can be true for babies and young children.

'Containment' is a helpful term for the way in which a mother (or mother-figure) can accept and hold a child's pain, anxiety or anger at a stage when the child is finding it overwhelming. Containment also involves not losing those feelings for the child, but making them accessible later in a form in which the child can deal with them. This is what Mum was helping Lily to do when they were looking at the photographs.

The way in which mothers ensure that the distance between themselves and their children is not too great in times of difficulty is a primitive aspect of maternal caregiving described by Bowlby (1969, pp. 409–510). Physical 'holding' – previously referred to in Chapter 1 – is often accompanied by kind of mental holding, sometimes referred to as containment. These ideas are akin to Bowlby's theory of attachment, which has been helpfully elaborated by Holmes (1993).

Erikson (1950, p. 200) reminds us that adults, when traumatised, tend to solve their tension by 'talking it out', and writes of 'the protective sanction of an understanding adult'. He suggests that for children, 'playing it out' with the undivided attention of an understanding adult is the most natural self-healing measure childhood affords.

It is important that, alongside nourishing and sharing the love and pleasure that children need, we also accept normal bad feelings. However, acceptance of 'bad' feelings does not have to involve unconditional acceptance of 'bad' behaviour (see Chapter 8).

Experiencing manageable feelings of loss, pain and frustration is most important. Growing up involves coming to terms with these things. We cannot hope to help children to manage their pain, fear and anger unless we are willing to try to understand their feelings. D.W. Winnicott (1964, p. 186) suggests that parents need enlightenment about underlying causes. We cannot hope to understand feelings unless we are willing to accept that the feelings exist and that they are important. The key is acceptance.

4

Adults accepting bad feelings

– THE BISCUIT BATTLE –

❛Joe is so cross. He's cross with all of us, but especially with Mum. He's being a real pain in the night, always climbing into their bed and wanting to be fed. Mum says she's beginning to feel like a walking dummy, and it's time to sort Joe out. That's why Joe is so cross with her, because for once Mum's not doing exactly what he wants. When things went wrong before, he used to sound all despairing and abandoned, and it made you want to give him a huge cuddle; but now that he's angry, it's as if he doesn't want us, and that really hurts.

Today there was a big fuss about biscuits; Joe wasn't just pointing or whinging, he was being really bossy. Mum had already given him two, and he hadn't even eaten the second one. When she said, 'No, two is quite enough,' he shrieked and flung himself backwards. When she tried to pick him up and distract him, he went on throwing himself around and took absolutely no notice of anything she tried.

Mum was really patient with him until Lily came in, but the first thing Lily said was, 'Can I have a biscuit?' I don't know if she knew that was what Joe was fussing about, but she might have, and they often gang up on Mum now. Anyway, Mum said, 'No you can't,' really crossly, and Lily was wailing, 'But I'm hungry', and Mum nearly dropped Joe when he went all stiff and flung himself backwards again. Then the phone rang, only the two of them were making such a noise you could hardly hear it. Mum just dumped Joe on the floor and told Lily to go in the kitchen while she answered it. You'd think Mum had been knocking them about, the noise they were making.

Anyway the minute Mum answered the phone, she asked the person to hang on. Then she went straight and fetched the biscuits and put them on the floor by Joe, so Lily could reach them too. That shut them up! Mum told me afterwards that it was Lily's new nursery on the phone and she didn't know what they'd think if they heard the children crying like that. Then she said something about Joe winning yet again, and he'd better not make a fuss like that at Gran's.

Mum says she hates it when Joe's furious and resentful, and partly what she hates are her own feelings when he's like that. She says it makes her feel useless and *unwanted and also like hurting him back, and then she feels ashamed of herself for even feeling like that. I've noticed that she gets extra busy when that happens, rushing about so she hasn't got time to think. It wouldn't be so bad if she wasn't so tired; she says she can't remember what it's like not feeling tired. I used to think it would be wonderful to have a baby like Joe, but now I'm not so sure. I'd have to be strong enough to love him even when he was being a little monster. That's what their dad calls him sometimes – 'little monster' – but he mostly says it in such a loving voice; it's only now and then he sounds as if he means it.* **9**

As well as feeling love and pleasure, it is normal for people to feel pain, anxiety and anger

Uses and abuses of distraction

This mixture of feelings may be further complicated when we consider our children's feelings alongside our own. We can look at not only our reactions to those of our 'important children', but also our reactions to our own feelings. It may be that sometimes we take our love and pleasure for granted, not acknowledging how we feel to the people concerned. In the study about self-perception already mentioned (Roberts, 1993), the children thought that what their parents most approved of at home – as well as outside the home – was obedience, politeness and conformity. However, the parents said that – at home – they placed most value on affectionate behaviour, with a willingness to learn being almost as important as 'social acceptability'.

Somehow those parents were accepting their children's love and affection without letting them know how much it meant. The study showed a sample of children struggling to be obedient and polite in order to gain their parents' approval, when what the parents said they wanted most was hugs and cuddles. Dealing with normal 'good' feelings involves acceptance and acknowledgment too.

It is hard for children to deal with feelings of frustration, pain and loss unless we, their important adults, are willing to acknowledge the existence of those feelings. Very often, however, it is much easier to distract a child – or indeed ourselves – from those feelings than to accept them and think what to do about them. There is no doubt that distraction can be an extremely useful strategy (as used by Mum on page 34). But it can sometimes mean not only that you will 'live to fight another day' but also that on another day there *will* be a fight. Unfortunately, the more practice children have at such battles, both at home and at school, the better they get at them; and the longer their negative feelings go unacknowledged and unresolved, the more entrenched they become.

Dealing with our own feelings

What about our own feelings as 'important adults'? Many adults were expected to hide their fear and anger in childhood; if this was the case, and if displays of affection seemed to go unnoticed, how does it feel when our 'important children' want to display their feelings? People who, in the past, have had to develop ways of keeping their feelings to themselves, may find it especially difficult to acknowledge and accept the feelings of others, including children.

Returning to our own feelings, it can be hard to accept that sometimes we may be so tired, anxious or frustrated that we feel like hurting a child. The danger is that, if we do not accept that occasionally it is normal to *feel* like that, it becomes difficult to control those feelings or to deal with them appropriately. There are two steps to take:

- to look beyond how we feel, to why we feel like that;
- to make a distinction between how we feel, and what we do about it.

This distinction is discussed further in Chapter 8.

Referring back to the 'cycle' described in Chapter 2, it is imperative that we learn how to accept our 'important children's' feelings – both positive and negative – so that they grow up more able to deal with their own feelings and the feelings of others. For many parents, teachers and citizens, there is a sharp awareness of the ever-increasing need for greater acceptance and understanding between people and between groups. Here is a way to halt the escalating tendency to confrontation and violence; a way in which, in our families, our schools and our society, we might move towards a more peaceful world.

– LILY IN CONTROL –

❝ *Lily is trying hard to keep Joe in his place, and it's a real battle. When he was just a baby at least she knew where he was; now he's all over the place. I love the way she invents games to tie him down. Yesterday they had this game under the table, and Lily said Joe's place had to be right at the back in the corner and he wasn't allowed to move! I was really surprised how long he stayed there.*

Lots of the toys Lily loves these days are about fastening things together or putting things in their right places. She's got a special doll with lots of buttons and zips and things – I think it's supposed to be for teaching her how to manage her own clothes, but she loves it because she can tie it up tight, just like she's trying to tie Joe up tight. I wonder if the toy shops would sell more of those dolls if they were labelled 'This doll makes children feel better about their baby brothers and sisters' instead of 'This doll teaches children to manage their own clothes'.

Lily likes strapping dolls into her buggy and she puts them to bed very firmly too. I suppose there's a bit of her that knows that it's not kind to Joe, wanting to get rid of him or wanting him to stay a baby for ever in a safe place where he can't take things from her. She can't help feeling like that, but she knows Mum and their dad don't like it, so she pretends.

Mum understands, though. Yesterday when they had the game under the table, Joe cried in the end, because Lily wouldn't let him out. Mum had to rescue him and give him a cuddle and she was quite cross with Lily for what she had done. But I saw her giving Lily a cuddle as well afterwards and she was saying something to Lily about Joe being a nuisance. What Lily said shows how mixed up she feels about him. Instead of being glad that Mum understands, she said, 'No, he's not!' and started arguing about it!

Denied pain, anxiety and anger all undermine positive self-concept – these feelings are hard to acknowledge and manage unless they are recognised by others as normal and acceptable

Siblings

It is clear from listening to the discussions of parents and people who work with children that it is common for adults to be concerned about whether, and how much, sisters and brothers love or hate each other. Many studies suggest that children often feel both love and hate at once, with friendly cooperation on the one hand and rivalry on the other. Dunn (1993, pp. 113–17) says that the brothers and sisters under five in her study who frequently entered into conflict were also found to be more likely to attempt to share, help and cooperate. According to Dunn, it appears that there is a wide range of differences between pairs of brothers and sisters, and that some pairs are both quarrelsome and friendly playmates, others are low on both negative and friendly dimensions, while other pairs are high on one or other dimension.

The general message from these studies seems to be that there are no obvious 'norms'. Relationships between brothers and sisters are varied and complicated, and raise a host of questions for us all. In different cultures, for instance, are variations in parenting significant in the way that relationships develop between siblings? Or is the basis of early relationships rooted in realities which cross different cultures? It seems that there are no straight answers to these questions. Although many studies have shown negative, hostile aspects of sibling relationships, more attention is now being paid to the way in which brothers and sisters are very often 'attached' to each other and to the ways in which they share thoughts and jokes, fantasies and playthings – often as equal partners.

It is entirely normal for brothers and sisters to play well together *and* to ignore each other, to agree *and* to argue, to love *and* to hate each other. These things are the basis of much early learning. This is not to say that 'only' children are disadvantaged. They have the benefit of their unique position and a longer period with an uninterrupted pattern of relationship with their parents; although they may need to develop certain social skills later, in the wider context of nursery, playgroup or school.

– LISTENING TO LILY –

❛ I think Lily's getting ill – maybe it's the flu I had last week. When Mum was getting her dressed this morning, she was really worried about having her hair brushed. Usually she doesn't mind much, but today she was crying about it. Mum got round it by saying she was sorry, but they really had to do it, and how about a story afterwards? Lily said 'No . . . yes!' and then she was really patient so that was all right. Mum always keeps her side of the bargain, so Lily knew it was worth it.

The old lady who's just moved in down the road dropped in to see Mum this morning, and Lily wanted to show her the little camel she got from her dad last week. After the lady had looked at it, Lily wanted to go next door and show it to George and Kathleen. George is usually in the garden, and Kath always lets her have sweeties. Mum said no about this (we couldn't go when the lady was here) and Lily suddenly cried really loudly. It wasn't to get her own way but just because she wanted to go and knew she couldn't. It was just like the way she's suddenly sick when she's ill, except she was throwing up her feelings instead of her breakfast!

She was hanging on round Mum's neck while she was crying, and Mum was saying things like, 'I'm sorry' and 'Never mind' and rocking her. After a bit that seemed to work, and she stopped, and went off to play with the camel. It reminded me of when she was little and she burst a balloon right in her face by biting it; she was really frightened, but Mum was down on the floor with her straight away after the bang, and when she saw that Mum wasn't frightened, she decided maybe it wasn't so awful after all. Mum has to be there, thinking about her though; it doesn't work if she just takes no notice.

It's harder for Mum when Lily's angry. That time when Lily first went to Dan's mum all day, Mum went away quickly because she really didn't want to hear Lily fussing. Dan's mum said Lily had been fine all day but when Mum came back she was awful; she shouted and screamed and wouldn't put her coat on or do anything. In the end, Mum had to carry her home still screaming, and after Lily was asleep that night, I heard her tell their dad that she didn't know what was worse – feeling furious with Lily for making such a fuss in front of everybody, or feeling bad about not listening to her in the morning. Their dad said there is no point hanging about, if you're going to go, then go; but Mum said she thought Lily wouldn't have been like that if she'd been a bit sympathetic first, instead of just dumping her. It's when Mum takes no notice of how she feels that she minds.

Anyway after the lady had gone home this morning, Lily said she was tired, so Mum made her a bed on the old sofa downstairs with a blanket and a pillow. She's been asleep ever since, and we're all creeping around whispering. It's lucky Joe still sleeps in the morning. **9**

Babies and young children can manage pain, anxiety and anger more easily if they know that other people accept and sympathise with how they feel

---

Verbal protest

The hardest form of protest to deal with seems to be verbal protest. If a child is physically hurting another, or throwing things dangerously, we don't have to think too hard about our response; we need to stop the child's action, although we may have to think *how* to stop it. But verbal protest is more complicated.

Parents say that one of the most infuriating things to listen to is whinging. Should we take no notice? Try and be patiently understanding? Shriek with irritation? Or possibly all three in quick succession? Argument is another version of verbal protest that tends to 'wind us up'. It is very hard to win an argument effectively, even with a small child, without giving it your whole attention, which may indeed be exactly what the child is asking for. Other aspects of verbal protest, such as anger, rudeness and 'unrepentance', are liable to feel like rejection to the listener; rejection is something even the most balanced person finds hard to bear.

For those people who were not allowed to protest as children and may not have had much practice since, verbal protest may be particularly hard both to listen to and to make. For them, it is more difficult to appreciate its value for the developing child and thus to tolerate it. People who were denied this way of accepting and dealing with their own feelings may not yet have found ways to accept, understand and deal with the sort of emotions that children's verbal protest evokes. In our role as important adults, we need to look for ways to break this circle. Some suggestions are made in the last section of this chapter.

Changes for children

As growing babies and children are learning to manage the changes in themselves, they also encounter a variety of changes in the world around them. Some of these changes may seem small to us, like growing out of the high chair and sitting on an ordinary one, or an older brother or sister starting school and therefore being out all day, but these things are major events for the young child. Other changes that may happen are major ones by any standards, such as a new baby, moving house, mum going to work or parents separating: these changes inevitably bring a host of lesser ones in their wake.

Of course, not all changes are bad, and a manageable amount of change is creative; but children get plenty of it in the normal course of events. As adults we know how stressful it feels when several big things in our lives are changing at once, and we don't feel quite in control of anything. This sensation is worth remembering when young children are faced with several major changes, or even one. Sometimes we are puzzled and worried by a child's behaviour, not realising that, for instance, moving house so that Gran comes to live with the family, as well as a new start at primary school, will have added up to 'a lot to cope with'.

One problem at a time

Usually there's not much to be done to avoid these changes, but sometimes it is possible to do something about the timing of them, from the child's point of view. It helps to aim for *manageable* change and to take things bit by bit. For instance, if Gran arrived a little while *after* the move to the new house, and if that move could be made a few weeks *after* the start of term, and if the reception teacher knows about what is happening at home, then those few months might contain a series of positive experiences for the child, rather than one long, overwhelming one.

This principle of 'one thing at a time' is a useful one to bear in mind if parents are separating. Children's parents, home, friends and school are four main areas of their lives. While the parent aspect is altering, it is important to try and keep the other three areas as unchanged as possible for a while.

Fathers

Much of this book may seem to focus on mothers, and it may appear like that because much of the subject matter – feelings and what to do about them – has traditionally been seen as 'women's territory'. We need to recognise and accept the crucial role of fathers as 'important people' also. A father can play so many roles, each one a different expression of his love for his child. John Lewis-Stempel's anthology of fatherhood (2001) is a timely reminder of the joys and pains of fatherhood down the centuries.

Expectations of and by fathers have changed radically during recent decades; the idea of the father as an occasional 'stand-in mother' has given way to a wider recognition of 'fathering' as separate and complementary to 'mothering', and of equally crucial importance in a distinct way. Both in their relationship with the mother as a co-parent and in their relationship directly with the child, fathers have a special part to play in the development of the child. For boys, the influence of the father as a role model (what he does rather than what he says) is very considerable, and it is the same with girls and their mothers (Holditch, 1992, pp. 6–65). This does not mean that fathers are less important to girls, or mothers to boys, but that the role modelling, although also important, may be less influential.

Accepting feelings, therefore, is an important issue for both parents as role models. Not only will girls *and* boys have a greater chance of learning to accept and manage how they feel, but they may be more likely to approach others, including their own children, in an accepting way.

Brazelton (1992, p. 423) writes:

All of the studies that measure the increasing involvement of fathers in their babies' care-taking point to the gains in the babies' development. Not only do school-aged children demonstrate significant gains in their IQ in families where the father was involved with them as infants, but they show more sense of humour, longer attention spans, and more eagerness for learning. These studies show that fathers who are available to their children enrich the child's self-image, and they also suggest that his involvement contributes to more stable family support for the child. A recent study demonstrates that father involvement gives the adolescent a surer sense of her inner 'focus of control' – the ability to resist peer pressure because she is sure of her own values.

The role of 'important person' is becoming increasingly complicated as new opportunities arise, dilemmas multiply and the world changes around us. As the pressures both in employment and in unemployment increase, and as the separation and divorce rates rise, more and more parents are having to make conscious decisions about spending time with their children. It is clear that, whatever the pattern of the family, fathers' involvement matters for children.

Easing distress

Here are three suggestions for making life easier when hurt, anxious or angry children need us at home, in nursery, playgroup or school:

1 Young children tend to carry on complaining or protesting until they feel they have been heard, even if it takes all day. A few minutes at the beginning of the protest spent listening carefully may be minutes well spent. Even if the problem remains unsolved, you may have stemmed the flow by accepting that the child's grievance is genuine, at least to him or her.
2 Bearing in mind that babies and children can manage better if they know that we accept how they feel, it's worth being openly sympathetic; adding sympathy to acceptance often reduces the pain, even if we cannot actually solve the child's

problem. This does *not* mean that you have to do what the child wants, unless that is what you decide.

3 If sympathy seems impossibly inappropriate (and it probably only works if it is genuine), a little detachment may help. This involves allowing the protest to continue while watching and listening really carefully. As babies' and young children's 'unreasonable' behaviour is almost always reasonable from *their* point of view, it may be possible to see or hear something with which to sympathise after all. Then suggestion number 2 has a chance.

If these suggestions seem to make no difference, do not be entirely discouraged. Very often children, and adults too, are profoundly affected by the close attention of another person, even if they cannot show it. Sympathetic acceptance certainly feels better than being ignored, even if the child is unable to acknowledge it at the time.

Miller (1992b, p. 52) writes:

> *The process whereby a child can convey distress to an understanding and receptive adult and be made to feel better is a most important one for the child's emotional development. As everyday experience tells us, 'a trouble shared is a trouble halved'. You cannot turn back the clock and make a child not have fallen over, and you cannot really abolish the fact that this gave him a nasty shock and a sore knee that will take time to mend. But you can understand how bad he feels, you can listen to his distress and you can absorb it. There will be times, of course, where the child is on his own. There will be times when grown-ups are busy or unsympathetic, or when they will deny or make light of his pain. But if he has enough experience of times when someone can bear his pain or worry with him, his own resources to bear distress will increase. He will feel as though he carries around in his memory and his imagination, consciously and unconsciously, helpful figures who will stand by him in his hour of need. This is how children themselves learn to be helpful and sympathetic.*

It is sometimes suggested that the best way to deal with a temper tantrum is to ignore it. The alternative of sympathetic acceptance may have more to recommend it. Sharing children's distress with them in a calm way, without fuss or panic, is one of the most effective things that 'important people' can do to help children grow up feeling good about themselves and other people.

POSTSCRIPT TO PART 2: FUNDAMENTAL FEELINGS

Living or working with young children? Questions to think about . . .

> ### As well as feeling love and pleasure, it is normal for people to feel pain, anxiety and anger

1. In your experience, what are the most common causes of pain for babies and young children? What causes anxiety? What makes them angry?

> ### Denied pain, anxiety and anger all undermine positive self-concept – these feelings are hard to acknowledge and manage unless they are recognised by others as normal and acceptable

2. How can we let children know that pain, anxiety and anger are normal for us too, without undermining their security?

> ### Babies and young children can manage pain, anxiety and anger more easily if they know that other people accept and sympathise with how they feel

3. What can we do to show very young children that we accept and sympathise with their difficult feelings?

RECOMMENDED FURTHER READING

For sharing with children . . .

Wishinsky, F. & Thompson, C. (1998), *OONGA BOONGA Big Brother's Magic Words,* **London, Picture Corgi**
Magic words or a magic relationship? Baby Louise keeps on crying, and all day no-one can help until her brother Daniel comes home from school with the magic words. But they don't work for anyone else . . . this wonderful book is full of love and humour.

For a good read . . .

Harris, P. (1989), *Children and Emotion,* **Oxford, Basil Blackwell**
Although written twenty years ago, this fascinating and thought-provoking book remains fresh, relevant and easy to read. There is a lot here about mixed feelings, for instance '. . . a situation that upsets one person may delight another and young children realize this . . . By the age of six, children grasp that the emotion displayed on one's face may not correspond to the emotion that one really feels . . .'

For reference . . .

Barnes, P. (ed) (1995), *Personal, Social and Emotional Development of Children,* **Buckingham, Open University Press**
If you need a comprehensive, reliable book in which to find out more about many of the issues raised in 'Self-esteem and Early Learning', this is it. Theories, issues and research evidence in developmental psychology are accessibly introduced. It includes examples drawn from case-studies, psychological research and practice, and activities that encourage the reader's active involvement.

PART 3

ABOUT OTHER PEOPLE

5

Children living with other people

– LILY NEEDS HER DOLLS –

❝ When I got home yesterday they were all out. I looked round the back but the garden was empty. Lily's and Joe's toys and shoes and clothes were lying all over the grass, and it was very hot and quiet. I sat on the swing and thought about being Lily. Sometimes she swings on the swing for ages. I wonder what she thinks about.

I heard her feet first. She came running round the corner of the house, with Mum and Joe just behind. Mum looked really hot and loaded down, carrying Joe with one arm, two dolls in a basket under the other and the picnic bag over her shoulder, too. They said they'd come to find me, and would I come with them to the park? Lily said everyone must go – Mum and Joe and her dolls and me.

'We'll just leave your dolls inside, they're too heavy to carry as well as Joe.' Mum was tired.

'Want my dollies to come.'

Mum's voice was patient.

'They're really too heavy – they'll be quite all right until we come back.'

'Want my dollies.' Her voice was even more determined than before.

'I really think they'd be better here.' Mum was nearly at the back door.

Lily's voice rose.

'I want everybody. I want my dollies too. I'll carry them.'

Mum turned around and came back. Without a word, she took them both out of the basket and gave them to Lily. Then she put the empty basket down on the grass, humped up Joe on her hip and led the way to the front gate. Silently Lily handed the dolls to me and followed her.

We walked down the road with Lily running ahead at a steady trot, with her head slightly down. After a little way she turned around and came back to us, drooping.

'Want a carry.'

Mum bent down and picked her up with her free hand, so that she had one on each hip. I offered to help, but Mum said they both seemed to need her at the moment, and she was quite well balanced with one on each side! Mum doesn't seem to mind things if Lily has a good reason, even if we don't know what the reason is. ❞

'Unreasonable' behaviour is almost always reasonable from the point of view of the baby or young child doing it

Other people's point of view

The opinion that 'unreasonable' behaviour can be reasonable, depending on your point of view, partly concerns the behaviour of other adults and children from the child's perspective, and partly concerns the child's own behaviour.

Babies and very young children are not generally able to think about another person's point of view, unless they can imagine themselves 'in that person's shoes' (Donaldson, 1978, pp. 17–31). They cannot understand what it's like to be an adult, although ideas are beginning to form as they gain experience in a variety of situations. Their ability to do this has been the starting-point of much debate (Bruner and Haste, 1987).

The tantrums of three-year-olds and the career choices of four-year-olds give some indication of how far they have to go! When Lily insisted on taking her dolls to the park, she didn't know how hot and tired Mum felt. She just knew that she needed her dolls for playing in the park. Yet often in matters that are directly relevant to them, young children show an awareness of what it's like to be the other person. Three- and four-year-olds sharing out biscuits usually display a very strong sense of justice! Sometimes a parent, at a loss as to the cause of the two-year-old's distress, will turn to the four-year-old for an explanation. Dunn (1988, p. 38) explores the extent of young children's early sensitivity to other people's feelings.

Generally, there is a reason for how someone is behaving which make sense to *them* (Bannister and Fransella, 1986, p. 65). Mum could have refused to pick Lily up on the way to the park, on the grounds that Lily had had a rest after lunch and couldn't really be tired; or she might have argued that Lily needn't be jealous of Joe, because Mum had carried Lily just as much when she was little, so she's had her turn. But that wouldn't have helped Lily to feel better. She just wanted a carry, and Mum knew that her wanting wasn't going to be reasoned away.

In discussing ways of handling aggression towards other children, Goldschmied and Jackson (1994, p. 201) make the following important point about the needs of the aggressor:

Although it is the child who has got hurt to whom we give our immediate attention as we intervene to stop the conflict and comfort the victim, it is important to notice how the aggressor is looking, which is often pretty unhappy. How we then relate to him (or her) also needs our understanding; there is little point in asking 'Why did you hit her?', a question to which a child is most unlikely to give an answer which has any meaning. Some kind of statement is more likely to be of help to the child, such as 'I know you're angry but you can't get what you want by hitting her – let's see what the trouble is'. In this way, the feeling is recognised but it is made clear that the action is not acceptable.

The sort of situation referred to here is one that tends to occur frequently between brothers and sisters. Although young children often seem to understand each other better than we understand them, there are many occasions when they do not. The situation is difficult enough for the child when an important adult will not accept his or her behaviour; but at least the adult can offer alternatives, distractions or limits that provide a sense of security. Seldom, though, would we hear one child say to another, 'Have this toy instead,' or 'Have I told you what I saw today?' or 'I'm not going to let you do that.' No wonder there is sometimes so much tension between children.

Children learn – often painfully – that other people don't automatically understand how they feel and what they want. It is part of the egocentric perspective not only to be oblivious of another's point of view, but also to assume that the other person is wholly conscious of yours. Mothers often manage to live up to this assumption to a remarkable degree in the first months and years; but in the process of widening their range of important people, it must come as a shock to many young children to find that this is very far from reality. No wonder they tend to struggle against the painful and bewildering realisation that the whole world, including their mother, does not revolve around them after all! Some children learn this reality quite quickly, especially those with brothers and sisters and confident parents; however, some may need special understanding and support when they come to playgroup, nursery or school.

Although it can be painful to find that other people matter too, this realisation makes life much more comprehensible for children. Learning to think about other people as well as themselves opens up the possibility that those people think about *them*, as well as themselves and other things. Once they understand that there *is* a reason for their important adults' 'unreasonable' behaviour, they in turn can 'deplore the behaviour', but not necessarily feel personally rejected.

– JOE'S TIGHT PLACE –

❝ *Lily's getting quite smart at knowing what's the matter with Joe, and how he feels. Not that she does much about it yet, though! But he seems to feel safe with her and maybe that's the reason.*

I had to stay home the other day so I was there all morning. Mum really knows what they like to play with; she came downstairs with Lily's dolls and a little pillow and the cover from the cot, and she just left them on the floor where Lily could find them. Lily couldn't wait to finish her drink; she put the pillow down on the floor near me and put the two dollies on the pillow. Joe was watching from his high-chair banging his biscuit on the tray and looking very sticky with his breakfast everywhere. Mum wanted me to change his nappy so we went upstairs. When I came back, Lily had got her dolls all tucked up under the cot cover really tight.

I sat down on the floor with Joe, and Lily came and sat beside me, but only for a minute; then she went and got her dolls and put them in a row next to us. I put Joe down at the end of the row too, and Mum said, 'One, two, three, four, five children in a row!' Lily looked really pleased; she likes things in their right places.

Joe didn't like it, though. He started crying and wanting to go back to Mum, and Lily looked resigned and furious all at the same time. She went over and sorted out the little pillow and cover again. She really wanted Joe to go to sleep on the doll's pillow; Mum didn't think it was a good idea, but Lily was so urgent about it that Mum gave in and put him down. He was quite happy for a bit, but then Lily tucked the cover around him very tight and rather near his face, and he cried. Lily held on to Joe really tight so Mum couldn't take him away but at the same time she looked up at us and said, 'Joe's worried', in a really understanding voice. She knew he didn't like it, but she wasn't going to let him go. The funny thing was, Joe didn't cry quite so loudly when she said that. **⁹**

> **It is possible to accept and sympathise with babies' and young children's pain, anxiety and anger without having to accept 'unreasonable' behaviour generated by those feelings**

Children's tolerance

One very positive aspect of young children is their ability to be tolerant and forgiving, especially with each other. This is often evident between children at nursery or playgroup, where they are making new friends and finding out how to get on with other people outside their family. For some children, this is a slow and difficult process, with much hurt and disagreement involved. Occasionally, others may stereotype such children as 'naughty' or 'rough', but it is astonishing how willing most children are to suspend judgment, and to accept, tolerate and support other children with difficulties, provided they have adult examples to follow, and support.

Sometimes things can be really hard for children on the receiving end of other children's anxiety or aggression, as well as hard, of course, for the one who is feeling anxious or angry. Unfortunately, because we would so much like to control or get rid of pain, anxiety and anger, our adult message is often, 'You're not really hurt,' or 'There's no need to be frightened,' or 'Don't be angry'. In other words, what we are saying is, 'Don't feel like that'.

If we can manage to allow children to keep their feelings, while at the same time being firm about what they are allowed to do, that helps them to be more accepting, but firm, both with themselves and with their more challenging friends.

Discipline and smacking

In the same way that children learn to allow others to have feelings by having their own respected, they learn much about ways of expressing disagreement by their own experiences of other people's reactions. It is an inescapable fact that they learn indiscriminately from our example. If only we could teach them to be selective about what they learn from us, taking no notice of the undesirable bits!

There is considerable disagreement in this country about smacking. Some people feel very strongly that smacking is a violation of children's rights; some argue that children need to be smacked in order to learn about the difference between right and wrong and grow up into responsible citizens; and others occasionally smack their children if they are feeling irritated. This last group varies between the two extremes of feeling profoundly guilty about it and wishing they hadn't, and not thinking twice about it. Discussions about smacking usually generate a lot of feeling, and our views are likely to be very influenced by our own experiences as children.

Quite apart from the 'rights' and 'wrongs', it is worth considering the things we want our children to learn as they grow up, and what children actually do learn from smacking. Most parents and teachers – and indeed governments – are anxious about the increase in crime and violence generally, and the way in which this affects their lives and the lives of their children. Consequently, their hopes for their children include the ability to get on well with others, learning to behave well and developing into responsible, law-abiding citizens. Most parents want their children to grow up knowing the difference between right and wrong.

Smacking can be a very effective short-cut to acceptable behaviour. The message to the child is clear and brief, and some children even seem to find a sense of relief in its use, as if it was actually needed. In fact, what is needed is a clear, firm message that means 'No'. Smacking is one way to give this message – often the easiest and most immediately effective way, which is why so many of us have done it. The real price for using it only comes later.

Children learn from what happens to them. If, when we *really* mind about something and need to say 'No', we smack, they learn that it is right to smack in those circumstances. And if they learn from experience that a smack is the answer to the slightest irritation, then when they themselves get slightly cross they will behave in the same way. Many children are thoroughly confused; they may have been told to stand up for themselves physically, by parents who have never learned to be assertive in any alternative way themselves. But they may have found themselves in trouble (even being smacked!) for hurting others, although this is how they are treated themselves.

It is important to bear in mind that there are enormous temperamental differences in children which are evident in the ways in which they perceive how we treat them. One child might experience a push as disturbingly violent, whereas another would be oblivious to it. It is, of course, not the case that all children who go through a patch of hurting others are being smacked themselves. It may be, however, that a child who begins to hurt others is struggling with something which does, to him or her, *feel* like violence.

In theory, there seem to be two clear alternatives. Either we go along with the use of physical punishment, in which case we must not be surprised or critical when children do the same; and we must be prepared for the fact that throughout their lives, the use of violence is liable to be – at least on first impulse – what they will do. Alternatively, we can find clear ways of saying 'No' that do not involve smacking: there are some suggestions about this in Chapter 8. This has the long-term advantage of giving children experiences of how to say 'No' themselves, without violence.

The trouble with this analysis is that, even after we have made a clear-cut decision either way, it is sometimes hard to be consistent. Even if we really think smacking is the answer, there may be times when we are not inclined to use it. On the other hand, if we take the dangers of using it seriously, there may still be times when our feelings get the better of us. Nevertheless, it is wise for a child's important adults to make a decision together, at least in principle. Children need a sense of direction about these things, and so do we. Then, if we find we've gone the wrong way, we can at least explain what happened: 'You deserved a smack for doing that, but I don't want to spoil our day, so this once you're lucky' or 'I'm sorry I hurt you. I didn't mean to, but you made me so hurt/worried/cross'.

Much has been said about children's need for acceptance. In relation to the way in which we react to young children's feelings and their behaviour, the balancing act here could be said to be something to do with discipline. It is about acceptance (of feelings) and the child's corresponding need for limits (on behaviour). Miller (1992b, pp. 32–3) writes:

> *Four-year-olds need people who make limits clear, who just won't allow them to behave in an extreme way and who don't see them as too powerful . . . boundaries must be drawn, or any child grows anxious. . . . Limits are necessary in all sorts of ways, and the successful setting of them is a relief to a child.*

Children need a structure within which to explore their world; they need people who are willing to say 'No' as well as 'Yes' calmly and consistently, so that they can feel safe enough to get on with learning. Setting limits successfully is not easy, but in this increasingly violent world we urgently need to find non-violent ways of saying 'no', that young children can both experience and practise. This is a very simple but important contribution that each parent and carer can make towards a less violent future. Practical strategies are discussed in Chapter 6.

– SHOPPING WITH DAD –

❝ 'Into the car everyone!' said the children's dad, 'We're going shopping.' Mum was out, and there was nothing for tea in the cupboard – not even chocolate biscuits! When we got to the shop, it was really quiet – everyone was watching the Grand National, Dad said. Lily rushed to get a trolley and Joe shouted and struggled to go in it. It was a long time since I had been shopping with them. There always used to be a fuss between them about riding in the trolley, but this time there wasn't, because Lily didn't want to anyway. She was too busy being grown-up and fetching things.

Their dad didn't know where to find things nearly as well as Lily did; at least, he pretended he didn't. Lily was really good at knowing where to look and at getting the right make and the right amount. The trolley got quite full up, what with the things for tea and some toilet paper and nappies and Joe as well. 'A logical collection,' their dad said. 'Tea an' toilet paper an' Joe – make a good ad for nappies, wouldn't it?' Lily laughed as well when I laughed, although she didn't get the joke; but it made her feel even more grown-up to be laughing all together. And Joe jigged up and down, and waved and shrieked – he loves being in the trolley because he's nearer the conversation!

Then we had a bit of a disaster. Lily was supposed to be looking for toothpaste and she was gone quite a long time. We'd got in the queue by then, but we were just going to look for her when she came round the corner, looking solemn. You could see something was up, just by looking at her. She took her dad's hand and dragged him off, saying, 'Had 'n accident' in her grown-up, very deep voice.

I stayed with Joe, and when they came back they both looked pretty serious. Dad said she had tried to climb up the shelves to reach 'the pink toothpaste', but all the toothpaste and plastic shampoo bottles had crashed into a heap on the floor. It had taken them a long time to put them all back.

'Can't think why we didn't hear the crash,' said Dad to Lily, when at last we were in the car. 'Sorry I wasn't there to catch you. That's what happens when you go climbing up shelves – lucky you didn't hurt yourself, wasn't it? But you remembered the chocolate biscuits!'

Then he turned round and grinned at her and she grinned back. ❞

Children learn to be responsible by taking responsibility

Using mistakes

Allowing responsibility is a tricky business. At the heart of the process is the question of whether the growing child will continue to *want* to take responsibility. Will the experience be sufficiently satisfying for the child to want to repeat it?

Our first and most important responsibility, as children and as adults, is for ourselves. We need to be able to be responsible for ourselves before we can take responsibility for other people and things. The more practice we have, the better we get at it. But we have to be careful about certain things if we want to be sure that our 'important children' continue to want to take responsibility – for themselves initially, and then in a wider sense for things, people and events in a variety of ways.

One of the most important things to be careful about is the need to keep the possibility of mistakes within safe boundaries. This means finding a balance between no possibility of a mistake (in which case the child may make no progress at all in learning to take responsibility) and the possibility of a very serious mistake (which might result in a determination not to risk anything so devastating again).

When things do go wrong, it is important that children feel safe to own up. This is not a moral issue, but a practical one about making sure that children do not give up the struggle of learning to do things for themselves, and for other people in a responsible way. It is absolutely crucial that children can risk mistake without fear of rejection. Genuine mistakes are, after all, only efforts gone wrong; nobody makes them on purpose. Children need to know that they will still be acceptable if they take responsibility for mistakes. Again, it is a matter of separating the child from the deed. If mistakes lead to disapproval and rejection, children will learn to avoid them, for disapproval and rejection are painful. But no mistakes means no exploring or trying anything unless children are sure they will get it right; and that rules out a lot of life and learning.

Some children learn not to admit disasters because they have found out that owning up is not safe – it hurts. The reason it hurts is because when someone rejects them, it makes them feel bad about themselves; this is the 'mirroring' process at work. After a while, a short-cut begins to occur whereby children feel bad about themselves when they make a mistake, even without any adverse comment from anyone else.

This is the start of a really slippery slope, the next step of which is not even to admit to themselves that something has gone wrong; they do this in order to avoid feeling even worse inside. Children – and adults – who really seem unable to admit even to themselves that they have made a mistake can be very difficult to get along with; but it is worth remembering that these people are hiding not only the mistake, but also a great deal of fear and pain. So allowing responsibility is indeed a tricky business unless we are prepared for children to make *manageable* mistakes and take responsibility for them, without fear of rejection.

Of course, it is important to be honest with children about the reality and significance of a mistake. They need to understand what has happened and why in order to learn from the experience. Some children make the same mistakes over and over again, and we sometimes attribute this to carelessness. But no one *wants* to go on making the same mistakes (unless it gives them satisfaction, in which case it's not a genuine mistake). These are the children who need help with recognising what is happening and why.

Learning from manageable mistakes is one of the most effective ways of learning, but it does need an element of reflection. This is something with which children may need adult help; some suggestions are made in Chapter 6.

Genuine praise

Another important factor in motivating children to take responsibility, is *genuine* recognition of their efforts and achievements. It really matters that we only give credit where it's due, and don't fall into the habit of praising on all occasions, 'to be on the safe side'. In fact, the safe side is just what it is not, as children who are praised indiscriminately soon come to suspect that all praise is meaningless. Instead of helping children to develop high self-esteem, this indiscriminate approach may have the opposite effect: it often fails to carry conviction at the time, and also prevents children from developing an 'inner yardstick' with which to evaluate their own efforts and achievements. Erikson (1950, p. 212) writes:

> *In this [the development of self-esteem] children cannot be fooled by empty praise and condescending encouragement. They may have to accept artificial bolstering of their self-esteem in lieu of something better, but their ego-identity gains real strength only from wholehearted and consistent recognition of real accomplishment, i.e. of achievement that has real meaning in the culture.*

Things are different then, for those children whose best efforts and achievements are consistently recognised. This is the way in which their positive self-concept develops, and it is positive self-concept which ultimately gives children that inner balance and confidence in their own ability which they need in order to make the very most of life.

Clearly, it is crucial that children feel safe to make 'manageable' mistakes and to 'own up' if they are to develop the ability to take responsibility for themselves and for other people and things. That their important people *realistically* recognise and value their efforts and achievements is also vital for their successful learning. Positive self-concept depends on recognising and valuing real effort and achievement.

6

Adults setting limits

– JOE'S CHANGED! –

❢ *When I came back from my holiday, Joe gave me such a surprise. He was bigger but it wasn't just that; he was more grown-up. At first I thought the biggest change was that he'd learned to crawl really fast; it meant he got around all over the place, instead of sitting there fretting. Mum and I knew if we didn't watch out, he'd hurt himself soon, particularly once he'd found out about climbing up on things, as well. He knows just what he wants and goes straight for it without stopping for anything – he goes so fast, too!*

When it came to tea-time that first day back, I could see there was another change as well. He'd got strong enough to be determined about things; not just about things he wants, but about things he doesn't want. I only noticed it when Mum went out suddenly because she'd forgotten to fetch something from the shop. She'd been in the middle of feeding Joe, one of his favourite green mushes she makes with left-over fish and peas. She pops another spoonful into his mouth as soon as he's swallowed the last one, and the first few mouthfuls go down really fast. But pretty soon he starts wanting to have the spoon himself and wanting to do it his way and then it goes all over the place – all over the table, on the floor – even in his hair! It reminded me of when Mum was feeding him herself and he used to take great gulps for the first bit and then start fooling around and wanting her to play.

Anyway they'd just got to the messy stage when she suddenly remembered about the shop, so she asked their dad to finish off with Joe; and then she was gone. That was when Joe got determined; he'd definitely had enough green mush, and then when his dad tried yoghurt, he only wanted two mouthfuls of that. What Joe wanted more than anything was to hold the spoon and do it himself, but his dad wanted him to eat some more without spreading it all around, so he kept trying. He gave Joe another spoon just to play with, but Joe still spat and dribbled and shouted and fussed; he wanted to do it all himself

In the end, his dad gave up. He said he wished Joe would eat his tea properly for once; he'd only be wanting it all over again in an hour or so. When Mum came back, Joe cried at her in a cross sort of way. It sounded like he was complaining about his dad not understanding that he'd had enough to eat and wanted to play.

And their dad had to read the paper twice as long as usual, to recover!

> ## 'Unreasonable' behaviour is almost always reasonable from the point of view of the baby or young child doing it

Two points of view

It could be said that it's all very well looking at the situation from the child's point of view, but what about our side of the picture? We're the adults. We know best.

It's helpful in this situation to remember that we don't have to give up our side of things, just because we've stopped to think about the child's side. What is important, though, is to let the child know that we *are* trying to understand. A change of perception on our part may well help us to be wiser in dealing with situations, but we may lose much of that advantage if we don't let children know about our efforts to understand them. The knowledge of our attention helps to give them a sense of security – or containment. That makes it easier for them to accept the adjustments we are asking them to make because of *our* point of view.

We may often ask ourselves why a child is behaving in a certain way and find that we have no idea of the answer. The inclination then, especially if this happens often, may be to give up trying to find the reason; it seems such a hopeless task. The thought that the child needs our acceptance anyway makes us all the more likely to grit our teeth and shrug our shoulders.

But there *is* a reason. Even though, if we knew what it was, it might seem extraordinary to us, nevertheless it would make sense to the child (although young children often do not have the words to explain the reasons for their feelings or their actions). Often, they don't really know what the trouble is themselves, or maybe they're too upset to explain it. Perhaps there has been a small (but important to the child) change in routine, or maybe something frightening has happened but no-one else has noticed. In playgroup or nursery, perhaps they don't know the adult well enough to talk about it. When this happens, we can only do the best we can for the time being, which is to assume that the fuss is about something that matters, even though we don't know what. We still don't have to give in – often we *can't* give in – but we can sympathise.

Reflective talking about problems

Children often encounter difficulties that blow over almost immediately, and it's best simply to let things take their course. Sometimes, though, we know that something more serious is afoot. Maybe a child's behaviour noticeably alters, with more tears, quarrels or clinging than usual. Perhaps the sleep pattern is upset, or bed-wetting happens a lot. We tend to try and talk about these things when they occur, but those are the very times when the child may be least able to help by telling us what the matter is. When a child is clutching us frantically around the knees or crying passionately as soon as we appear after an absence, he or she is in no state to say anything that is likely to make sense.

This is when it may help to think about when there *will* be a quiet time to talk. Young children – like the rest of us – do need regular times to think and talk about what has happened to them and how they feel about it. Choosing the right moment needs careful thought: certain times of the day which may be particularly suitable for some children – maybe meal-times, bath-time or 'last thing' – can be battle-grounds for others. In playgroup, nursery and school settings, a special time during the session for discussing events and feelings can be very valuable.

Once the passion has blown over, a child may respond to a gentle question, especially if we adults can be quite calm and relaxed about it. For instance, 'You remember when you didn't want me to go this morning? When you cried? Can you remember what the trouble was?'

Sometimes the answer is quite straightforward, but occasionally the reason is too complex for a straight answer, and children may invent reasons that they think we will understand. It is as well to be prepared for this possibility; after all, we tend to do the same thing ourselves to them!

Talking about things calmly after the event can work well as a way of unscrambling quarrels, too. An example might be, 'Do you remember when you hit Joe this morning? He must have made you very cross – what was the trouble?'

This sort of conversation gives us a chance to suggest ways of dealing with pain, anxiety and anger so that they do not escalate.

Probably most of us would say that we long for the day when our children will understand and accept that they do have to do certain things. Of course, children have trouble with different things in different places, and while some seem to be born with the ability to take life as it comes, others seem to be ready to struggle all the way (Reid, 1992, p. 12). Frequent difficult areas include eating, sleeping, getting dressed, sharing, waiting, listening, keeping still, being quiet, as well as a great many other things that we want children to do!

As adults, we have more or less learned that managing these things is essential, at least for most of the time, if we are to be acceptable to the people with whom we live. But young children don't know this. Until they begin to get the idea of taking responsibility for themselves, and until they begin to see things from another person's point of view, none of it makes much sense, and our insistence on these things is often very hard for them. It may help if we try not to ask for too much too soon and if we show that we want to understand what it feels like for them.

Being role models

Although our understanding often makes no difference to the outcome for the child, our attention to the causes of upsets is an important experience for children. Quite apart from the comfort of the moment, they are being shown a way of responding to other people that they may then learn to use for themselves. Then, when they are presented with *our* inexplicable demands, they may 'catch' the idea that there must be a reason, even if they can't understand it.

If this is true, then maybe we can show them something else, too, about looking for solutions. If *we* look for ways to compromise and to solve their problems, children may learn to look for solutions and accept compromises, too. This doesn't have to be a bargaining situation; perhaps more a case of us leading the way, with enough faith in children to know they will follow – in the end!

– EATING CUSTARD CREAMS –

❛ *I love watching Lily eating custard creams. I used to eat them like that, too. She takes the two halves apart, then she licks the cream off the insides and then she eats the boring outside bits – sometimes!*

This morning Lily had a dreadful cough, and Mum gave her a drink. After that, she opened a packet of Jammy Dodgers – they've got custard cream and jam in them as well – to cheer Lily up after all that coughing. Of course, when Lily had eaten the first one she wanted another; but Mum said if she really wanted another biscuit, she could have one of the other ones in the tin, but not another Jammy Dodger

'I want a cream one.'

Mum said, 'No more Jammy Dodgers' again.

'But I want to choose,' said Lily getting furious.

Mum quietly said yes, she could choose between a malted one and a Rich Tea one out of the tin.

Lily was nearly into one of her screaming fits, but I could see there was a bit of her that quite liked Mum being firm; it made her feel safe to have Mum saying 'No' calmly, even though it made her want to scream as well. Just then Mum remembered that the cats hadn't had their breakfast. Lily loves helping to feed the cats, so she forgot all about biscuits and rushed to find the cat food.

Later on, Mum and Lily had another argument, this time about the telly. Lily just loves that programme about the puppets on the boat, and she went and switched on the telly much too early and sat right up close to it watching a really boring programme about selling cars. Mum turned it off, saying Lily had watched the telly too much yesterday morning, and she didn't really want to watch the boring programme about cars, and anyway Dan was coming to play soon.

'But we haven't seen this and we want to, don't we?' Lily said, looking at me. Mum glanced at me rather crossly, and said, 'Oh no you don't, do you?'

Meanwhile, Lily had turned the telly on again. Mum said she'd be really angry if Lily didn't stop. Instead of turning it off, Lily got out her Thomas the Tank Engine video and said, 'Well, we do want Thomas the Tank.' She looked at me determinedly. Mum heaved a sigh.

'I'll tell you what,' she said. 'You put in Thomas the Tank and get it ready but you're not to press the play button until Dan gets here. OK?'

So Lily got it ready; then she found her whistle in the bottom of the big dish in the kitchen and blew it really suddenly and loudly so we all jumped!

It is possible to accept and sympathise with babies' and young children's pain, anxiety and anger without having to accept 'unreasonable' behaviour generated by those feelings

---

The need for limits

Adults living and working with children need to be able to offer acceptance *and* set limits, both at the same time. Children need security – both physical and psychological – to learn well, and this double security can only be achieved if we are consistent about the limits as well as the acceptance. An overdose of limits can eliminate confusion in the short term, but children then find it hard to take responsibility for themselves as they grow older.

On the other hand, real acceptance without any limits is frightening for children, and confusing too. Young children need to be clear about what is allowed and what is not; they need 'important people' who will not allow them to become too powerful or to behave in an extreme way (Miller, 1992b, pp. 28–33).

Developing self-discipline

One of our aims for children is likely to be that, ultimately, they grow out of the need for external limits and learn to regulate their own behaviour. This is another reason why acceptance and understanding are an important part of the picture. Children who have not been encouraged to think about how to behave in relation to what they want to do may well be good at doing as they are told; but sooner or later comes the time when they must think for themselves. Unexpected situations arise – more frequently as children grow older – when the rules don't seem to fit and there is no one to ask.

We cannot be there every minute of the day for ever. Children need to be developing an inner core of common sense upon which they can begin to rely. An important part of this common sense is their internalisation of their important people. In effect the child learns to think, 'What would mum/dad/my teacher have said?' So if we only say 'yes' or 'no', and if we don't do much honest explaining, we may leave children with very little to fall back on for themselves. They may be in a situation where, with no internal limits of their own, they must look elsewhere for rules. In adolescence there will be no shortage of alternatives, either: peer-group pressures and role models from videos and the television are two particularly powerful possibilities.

Establishing our priorities

If we want children to keep their balance in the face of these pressures, we must get in first, in early childhood; we must be willing to explain and discuss how we feel and why we do things. It helps to be clear, both to ourselves and to our children, about our priorities. Of course, it's really important that, for example, children know they must not run into the road without looking, and most children of four will say that hurting someone is wrong, although they may not know why. But finding out about what is allowed and what is not can be a confusing business for young children. Apparently it's fine to get in a mess making mud-pies at playgroup in the morning, but not in the garden at home in the afternoon just before Gran arrives. It seems to be clever to make squiggly patterns with crayons all over the clean new book that Gran brings, but it's not all right to do it all over the not-so-new wallpaper in the bedroom. It's grown-up to mix flour and sugar and things when Mum's there to tell you how, but it's naughty to do it on your own.

We have a lot of listening and a lot of explaining to do. It helps children when we make a distinction between those things that *really* matter to us – like not running into the road and not seriously hurting people – and those things that are not of absolute importance yet, although we hope they will come to understand these soon. Whether they are at home or out, children need to know clearly which the important rules are.

When everything seems to be going wrong, it may be over-optimistic to try and put it all right at once. When it feels as though there's only one word in the language – 'no' – we can be sure that we are asking too much. No one can change everything they do all at once, especially not a young child; but maybe they can change one thing. Perhaps other things will right themselves, and if not, we can always tackle them later. The important question is, which thing should we concentrate on? When so many things seem to need sorting out, where is it best to start?

It can be helpful to talk this over with another adult; we sometimes get a better picture of what is happening that way. It helps to choose one thing that can solve other problems, too. For instance, if we are firm about putting the reluctant toddler to bed at a regular time and with a regular routine, that may be good news for older children who are needing their own time with us too, especially since the toddler was born.

Being consistent

It's hard enough for children to learn what is allowed and what is not in the normal course of events. We sometimes make it even harder for them by failing to be consistent about the rules. If children know that they're not allowed to eat in the front room, except when they can get away with it because mum and dad are too busy or tired to notice, then they never quite know whether today is one of those days or not; and if they are given an extra cuddle on Tuesday and sent to their bedroom on Wednesday, both because of arguments about sharing toys, what can they make of that? It would be unrealistic to expect that we can *always* be consistent in our reactions, but the more consistent we can manage to be, the more likely children are to be clear about what is allowed and what is not.

Another important aspect of consistency is that sooner or later children are going to discover about different values and priorities, even amongst their 'important people'; they are then faced with choices, uncertainty and opportunities to manipulate. We may be splendidly consistent as individuals, only to find that considerable confusion is caused by our failure to agree a common view with the child's other 'important adults'. It can be particularly helpful for staff in playgroups, nurseries and schools to bear this point in mind; children are likely to feel more secure where staff work as closely as possible with families so that similarities and differences can be identified and, if possible, discussed.

Sometimes, though, no amount of discussion achieves common ground, and the only course of action open to a child's 'important people' seems to be to agree to differ. When this happens, one way for everyone to help the child is to be open about the differences. For instance, 'I know Dad doesn't mind you bringing your bike in here, but I do, so please will you take it out again now?' or 'Mum wants you to stand up for yourself, doesn't she? So do I, but the way we do it at school is by talking, not hitting. . . . Have you tried saying, "No, don't do that"?'

Another form of inconsistency that is less straightforward is the one about treating individual children differently. Children are generally very quick to let us know when we are doing this, but they do need to learn that individual children, at different stages of their lives, need different rules. It is possible to be fair without treating children identically; indeed, it can be argued (and often is, by older children) that to accord the same privileges at the same time is most unfair.

Behind the child's 'It's not *fair*' is really the cry 'You don't love *me* as much'. Surely no 'important person' in the world is immune from this cry and from the guilt it generates. Privileges and presents do not solve it, though; in fact, they may even confirm the child's suspicion that we have something to feel guilty about. If there is an answer, it lies in 'unconditional acceptance' (described in Chapter 1) and the combination of efforts to understand our important children, together with calm, firm setting of limits.

Temper tantrums

Temper tantrums are extremely common in very small children. It is estimated that nearly twenty per cent of two- and three-year-olds have a tantrum at least once a day, with a much higher proportion having the occasional tantrum (Goldschmied and Jackson, 1994, pp. 200–1). As very small children have such a high level of frustration, together with such a limited command of language, this is not at all surprising. Goldschmied and Jackson's advice, (1994, p. 201) is particularly helpful:

> *At moments like this, it is clear that words are quite useless, in fact any attempts to check the tantrum generally make things worse.*
>
> *The most helpful thing for the adult to do is to stay near the child, perhaps sitting down, attentive and available but not intervening until the child is quiet again. It is often noticeable that other children watch very carefully and are reassured that [the adult] stays calm and, once the tantrum has passed, helps the child; with a drink of water and quiet words, to feel all right again.*

Goldschmied and Jackson also mention that some children who have frequent tantrums may have learned that this is the best (or only) way to get what they want, and that we should try to avoid reinforcing this behaviour. Although sometimes tantrums seem to occur without any warning, quite often we can see them looming all too easily. Brazelton (1992) proposes talking about an issue with the child before things go too far: presenting choices and explaining the way we would like the child to behave. He suggests that, if we definitely want a child to do something, we should never ask, 'Will you?' but instead should say 'Now it's time.' Penelope Leach's thoughtful section on tantrums (1997:376–9) reflects her wisdom and experience and repays careful reading.

Finally, the 'Learning Together with Twos' video in PEEP's Learning Together Series (2000) contains a powerful section showing how parents in different families manage their children's tantrums.

Television and videos

The impact of television and videos on young children is enormously important. The results of television viewing can have a major effect on their development, their consciousness and their learning (Singer and Singer, 1990, pp. 176–98). Although it can be argued that there are benefits for children in watching television, it may be appropriate to set some limits about what children watch and for how long. The increase of television sets in children's bedrooms is deeply worrying.

In households where the television remains on throughout the day, babies have difficulty in learning to distinguish their mother's voice from other voices. Turning the TV off sometimes, even if only for half an hour, can make a difference provided someone spends that time talking and playing with the baby.

The debate about the impact of television needs to be placed firmly on to the agendas of all those places where children live their lives. We need to gain information, discuss appropriate responses and act. Meanwhile, it is a good idea to join children in their viewing as much as possible. This way, we can help children to begin to develop the important ability to look critically at programmes and films, and learn to discuss them. Then, rather than the possibility of an isolating, frightening or confusing experience, watching can become a social event.

– DAN STAYS THE NIGHT –

❝ Lily's friend Dan came to sleep last week. His mum and dad were going to see his gran, and his mum thought he'd be better with us. It was the first time he'd slept the night away from home, and Lily and Dan had such a good time that now Lily wants to go and sleep with him; Mum says maybe, one day.

Dan arrived at bath-time, so they scampered off upstairs. You should have seen the bathroom after that! Mum said Dan's the bravest bath-swimmer she's ever seen. Lily has just learned to put on her own pyjamas, and she promised to help Dan if he was good, and no grown-ups were allowed. When they came out of the bedroom, it was hard not to laugh because they looked so solemn and funny; Lily's pyjamas were inside out, and Dan's bottoms were on upside-down. They were pleased to have managed on their own, but I think they guessed that things weren't quite right. Mum says we mustn't laugh when Lily makes funny mistakes, otherwise she'll stop trying, so we managed to be serious and say how clever they were to manage to get them on.

Mum let them lay the table for tea, too. They were so proud of themselves when they'd done it all. Dan even remembered the salt and pepper. Lily said 'What about flowers?' and that was where the trouble started.

Mum gave Dan a little pot and said they could pick three flowers each out of the back garden. Lily liked that, because she knows how many three is. They rushed off together and a minute later we heard a crash.

'Oh no,' groaned Mum. 'I knew I shouldn't have given them that one.'

Outside, Lily was looking at the smashed pot, and Dan was nowhere to be seen.

'Dan dropped it,' Lily said. 'Can we have another one?'

'Where's Dan?' asked Mum.

'I don't know,' said Lily. 'Behind the shed.'

They went down the garden to Lily's favourite hiding place behind the shed. Dan was there, looking a bit flushed.

'It was Lily', he said.

'What was Lily?' asked Mum.

'Lily dropped it.'

'No, I didn't,' said Lily indignantly

'It's all right, Dan,' said Mum, holding out her hand. 'Let's go and pick up the pieces.'

'I didn't do it. She did it,' he insisted.

'No, I didn't,' said Lily again hotly.

Mum looked at them thoughtfully.

'It's hard to say it's your fault if you think you're going to get into trouble,' she said to no one in particular. 'Let's not worry about who did it just now. Perhaps we'll talk about it later.' She walked back towards the house.

'Who's going to find three flowers for the table?' she asked over her shoulder.

When Lily's dad came back, he thought the table looked wonderful, especially the flowers in the egg-cup.

'We did it,' they shouted, jumping round him.

Tea-time is always special, because everyone's together and it's the best time to talk about things. Sometimes Joe fusses or makes an awful mess, but he's learning; he wants to be big like Lily, so he copies her. Dan wanted to get down and play because they don't have tea together in his house; but when Mum and Lily's dad started talking about how they caught the burglar last summer, he changed his mind. I think they did it on purpose – Dan always wants to talk about burglars.

Then we talked about breaking things and having accidents and what upsets people. Lily said she hates it when people say she did something when she didn't. I don't know if she was thinking about Dan or if she had forgotten and was saying it anyway. Dan said he hates it when grown-ups are cross, and Mum said she might be sad if someone had an accident with something precious, but she wouldn't be cross. Then Dan said he had had an accident today when he dropped the pot, and Mum said it was really grown-up and sensible of him to tell her about it. When she said that, Dan looked really pleased and happy

Dan and Lily didn't go to sleep until very late; I think they tried but it was too exciting. In the end, Mum got a bit cross with them because she was afraid they would wake up Joe. **9**

Children learn to be responsible by taking responsibility

Encouraging independence

The first form of responsibility that means something to young children is the responsibility for looking after themselves. There are all sorts of ways in which we can encourage them to learn to be independent and to take responsibility for themselves, and the achievement of each small step, together with our recognition of it, gives them the satisfaction and motivation to tackle the next

Some of the areas that tend to cause most tension in the early years – eating, sleeping, toileting, clothes and siblings – also contain particular opportunities for growing independence (see Chapter 5 for ways of using children's mistakes positively and giving genuine praise when appropriate). These are ways in which children can be supported and encouraged towards independence.

When children are having trouble with eating or sleeping, when they can't seem to get the hang of using the toilet, or when they seem to spend the whole day quarrelling with a brother or sister, they may need the safety of 'no blame' in these areas in order to make progress. We adults know what it feels like to get blame rather than sympathy for a mistake we never meant to make, and how readily we resolve never to risk *that* again! However, it's often hard for us not to blame young children when we so often find ourselves dealing with the consequences; and, of course, it's important to involve children in the consequences of their mistakes, too, in a positive and sensitive way. Our reward for resisting blaming them as well comes in the shape of children who will always be willing to 'have a go'.

Recognising real achievements

Families, playgroups, nurseries and schools need a culture of recognition and acceptance, not only of mistakes, but of successes too. This is something about which 'important adults' can lead the way, although it seems that many of us find it hard. We tend to be much more aware of our failures than our successes and often find it uncomfortable and rather embarrassing to own up to our achievements.

Our embarrassment can rub off on the children who live with us, in the same way that other attitudes do, but there is no need for this to happen, once we are aware of it. Realising our power as role models, we 'important adults' can help in families and other places where children live their lives, by being open about our own efforts and achievements, and by noticing and praising each other. It is worth making a habit of recognising, accepting and celebrating success, in ourselves, in each other and in our young children.

However, there is a pitfall to watch out for here. Curry and Johnson (1990, pp. 91–2) emphasise that making a habit of celebrating success only works if the successes are real; and that heavy doses of well-intentioned but often empty praise can be counter-productive. The need to praise children appropriately for genuine effort and real achievement means that we need to know a lot about levels of understanding and their skills. Only this way can we appreciate the extent of their efforts and achievements and recognise 'true accomplishments'.

Parents are the experts in relation to their own children and know by living with them day by day when they are making efforts and when they are achieving. Adults in early-years settings will know about child development generally, but can usefully develop ways of working together with parents in order to know more about individual efforts and achievements (Whalley, 1994, p. 56). We need *accurate* knowledge about children, and this highlights the necessity for effective methods of observing, assessing and recording children's progress (Bartholomew and Bruce, 1993, pp. 1–6).

It may seem contradictory to find so many suggestions about success and praise in a chapter about setting limits; this, though, is the other side of the coin – the important *context* for success in calmly, firmly and consistently setting the limits young children need.

POSTSCRIPT TO PART 3: OTHER PEOPLE

Living or working with young children?
Questions to think about . . .

> **'Unreasonable' behaviour is almost always reasonable from the point of view of the baby or young child doing it**

1. Think back to a time when a child was behaving 'unreasonably'. What might have been the reasons?

> **It is possible to accept and sympathise with babies' and young children's pain, anxiety and anger without having to accept 'unreasonable' behaviour generated by those feelings**

2. Are you aware of consistent patterns of 'unreasonable' behaviour? From a starting point of acceptance and sympathy, is there anything to be done to avert them?

> **Children learn to be responsible by taking responsibility**

3. What are some of the practical ways in which very young children can be offered genuine responsibility?

RECOMMENDED FURTHER READING

For sharing with children . . .

Burningham, J. (1973), *Mr Gumpy's Outing*, London, Puffin Books
This picture book is a classic, for very good reasons. Mr Gumpy takes the children, the rabbit, the cat, the dog, the pig, the sheep, the chickens, the calf and the goat for a day out on the river. They fall in, climb out, and trek home across the fields for the sort of tea we all dream about. Dignified lovable Mr Gumpy knows all about acceptance.

For a good read . . .

Paley, V. (1992), *You Can't Say You Can't Play*, London, Harvard University Press
Peer acceptance or rejection in the early years of school makes a profound impact on self concept. Vivian Gussin Paley's enchanting, inspiring and optimistic book is about social relations among young children. It is beautifully written, with accounts of children's deliberations and Magpie's fairy-tale adventures interwoven to highlight the issues of exclusion in early childhood.

For reference . . .

New Zealand Ministry of Education (1996), *Te Whariki Early Childhood Curriculum*, Wellington, Learning Media
This inspirational and challenging bicultural early childhood curriculum is founded on the following aspirations for Maori and non-Maori children: 'to grow up as competent and confident learners and communicators, healthy in mind, body and spirit, secure in their sense of belonging and in the knowledge that they make a valued contribution to society.' The principles – empowerment, holistic development, family and community, and relationships – are woven together with the strands of the curriculum – well-being, belonging, contribution, communication and exploration – as a structure for the goals of child development. This woven 'mat' is the basis for appropriate curriculum content in individual settings.

PART 4

LINKING WITH LEARNING

7

Children's ways of learning

– GOING TO NURSERY SCHOOL –

❝ The other day Mum got a letter from the nursery school. It said that after Christmas, Lily can go every day in the mornings, and would she and Mum like to come and visit sometimes? Mum said, 'What a good idea', but then she thought that, as Joe might be a nuisance and swallow things, perhaps I could take Lily instead of her. When she explained this to the school, they said it was quite all right about Joe, and they like having toddlers around. But Mum said she'd worry about Joe anyway so I'd better go for most of the visits. We all went the first time, though: Lily and Joe and Mum and me.

Lily had a great time. They had all her favourite things – painting and drawing and cutting and glueing – and lots of things to play with in the garden. She did a special painting for her dad. She said it was him in bed, and you could see where his head was, and she did Toby on the bed too. She said he was purring because her dad was cosy. Mum was just saying how lovely it was, when Lily started putting black paint all over the top of it. Mum said, 'Don't spoil it,' but Lily wouldn't stop. She said it was night-time and she was painting the dark!

There were two other children with their mums there as well, but they had done lots of visiting already. You would have thought that Lily was the old hand, though, and they were the new ones. Mum got talking to one of the other mums, and apparently her little boy Daniel hadn't played much with other children before they came to nursery. He spent all the time as near to his mum as he could get. The trouble was, his mum thought it would be best if she left Daniel to get on with it. I heard her say to the teacher that she thought it was time for her to go, but she knew he would make a fuss, so she was going to go without telling him. The minute she said that, the teacher stopped what she was doing and they had a talk about it.

The teacher said it would be a bad idea to go away without telling Daniel. She was very nice, but very definite about it. She asked if the mum had ever gone away without telling him before. The mum said she had, and that apparently he'd made a big fuss when he'd found she'd gone, but he'd stopped crying quite soon. She asked why it was a bad idea. The teacher said because then he'd never know when she might disappear. It would make him worry and want to hang on to her all the more. She said children usually stopped crying after their mums or dads have gone because there's no point in crying then – it doesn't bring them back. It doesn't always mean they feel better, though. The teacher said that it would be best if the mum promised Daniel that she wouldn't go without telling him – then he could get on with playing without worrying.

In the middle of this, Daniel suddenly came and grabbed his mum round the knees – he must have noticed her talking to the teacher and guessed they were talking about his mum going. The mum looked rather desperate and said how was she ever going to leave him then. The teacher said that if she promised not to go without telling him, then Daniel would feel safer with her still here and he would soon realise that it's safe without her as well. He would stop worrying enough to see that the teacher looks after children all right until their mums come back.

There was another mum who couldn't leave her child either. It was when mum took Lily to find the toilets that I noticed them. The little girl was called Kimberley, and her mum helped her a lot. I heard Kimberley say she wanted to do a painting; if Lily had said that, Mum would have said things like 'OK' and 'Don't forget to put on an apron' and 'Can I see it when it's finished?' and maybe even 'Can I come and watch?' This mum hovered around sorting out the apron, choosing the colours and fussing about the paper: Then, when Kimberley said she wanted to go out, she had to just stand there while her mum changed her shoes and put on her coat for her. After all that, she wouldn't go out without her mum coming with her, so there was a long wait while her mum got dressed too.

I thought that Kimberley wouldn't ever learn how to do things herself because she didn't need to, with her mother doing them for her all the time. Perhaps the mum didn't really like the idea of Kimberley managing without her. If the mum thinks Kimberley won't be able to manage on her own, maybe Kimberley will think that too. Then she'll think she can't do things, instead of knowing she can.

Lily told her dad all about her new nursery at tea-time. She gave him the black painting and she had to tell him all about what was under the black paint because it was dark. Then she remembered some things at the nursery that Mum and I hadn't even noticed, like the milk they drink out of little bottles and the boy called Michael who played with her in the garden. There was a really big cardboard box, and they had both got inside and pretended it was their house.

When her dad asked, 'What are you going to do when you go next week?' she said, 'Pretend with Michael'. 〝

Learning involves struggle and adjustment. Too much struggle is overwhelming. Too little struggle means no adjustment

Children learning

Young children – and adults too – learn well with an appropriate level of challenge; this is more helpful than overwhelming demands on the one hand, or nothing with which to struggle on the other. Piaget's theoretical model of adaptation, in which he describes 'accommodation' and 'assimilation' (Piaget, 1953, pp. 407–19), suggests a model for the way in which learning takes place. The work of Athey has done much to illuminate our understanding of Piaget's thinking. She shows (1990, pp. 75–6) that the way in which we learn ranges from struggle and practice to play:

> . . . new knowledge is associated with struggle and well-assimilated knowledge is usually accompanied by feelings of confidence (competence generates confidence). 'Playfulness' signifies knowledge that is so well assimilated that it can be played with.

Elaborating on Chukovsky's idea (1966, pp. 96–8) that it is only when a child knows something very well that he or she can play with it, Athey gives the example of the game of 'Ring-a-ring of roses'. When toddlers fall down, they are usually furious because falling down means failure to stand up, whereas slightly older children, who are having fun with pretend falling down, are signifying real competence in staying upright. Struggle indicates new knowledge, whereas playfulness indicates well-assimilated knowledge.

Bruce (1991, p. 34) uses the diagram below to illustrate the relationship of the terms 'accommodation' and 'assimilation'.

accommodation				assimilation
struggle	practice	play	humour	bored

Working together on the Froebel project (Athey, 1990, p. 76), Athey and Bruce recorded different kinds of children's responses in the project environment. They discovered that over eighty per cent of responses were accommodatory (surprise, perturbation, struggle, absorbed or focused attention) and – unexpectedly – that only slightly more than five per cent of responses were assimilatory, showing playfulness and humour. A possible explanation for this was thought to be that the stimulating environment of the project generated struggle and other accommodatory responses.

However, as it is well-assimilated knowledge that stays in the mind and continues to be of use, this finding raises questions about what constitutes the very best learning environment for young children. It is often suggested that what children need is plenty of stimulation; but, although stimulation is clearly important, perhaps we should not lose sight of the need for a balance. If we want long-term benefits from early childhood education, and if we value the development of imagination, creativity and originality in young children, it will be important to include in the learning environment many opportunities to play and be creative with those things with which children are already familiar.

In Lily's nursery, the boy called Daniel whose mother wanted to 'leave him to get on with it' was overwhelmed. He had little experience of playing with other children, and so had few ideas to 'hang on to' in the new situation. In addition to that, his previous experience of his mother leaving him had been too bewildering to be of use to him in the new situation. His mind could not accommodate the unthinkable possibility of being in the nursery with so many unknown children and adults, and without his mother. Lily, on the other hand, knew a lot already about how to make new friends, and had learned that mum is both predictable and reliable about going away and coming back; she doesn't go without telling Lily and she comes back when she says she will. Because of this, Lily could manage the new situation by building on previous experience, whereas Daniel's experience was too limited or too negative to help him.

Kimberley, whose mother wanted to do things for her all the time, was also having difficulties. With few challenges, there was little opportunity for her to add to her existing knowledge and understanding. Neither did she have the opportunity to adjust her current knowledge and understanding in the light of new information. This is the reason for the early education principle that, with all new learning, it is essential to 'start with the child'. New ideas or experiences make sense to children if they can be 'attached' to previous relevant experience.

Manageable experiences

There needs to be some sort of challenge or tension for learning to take place. If nothing is new or challenging, then nothing changes and we make no progress. The mother in Lily's nursery who didn't let her child do things for herself was getting in the way of the child's learning. We tend to think that total absence of stress is the ideal state: no quarrels to resolve, no problems to overcome, no difficulties to face. Such a state may seem wholly desirable, but it is uncreative. It is a manageable level of struggle which constitutes the most exciting, satisfying and fruitful situations in terms of learning. A good early childhood education setting where children learn effectively will be physically, socially, emotionally and cognitively interesting and challenging.

If left to their own devices, children in play automatically regulate their own levels of challenge. On the one hand, too little challenge leads to boredom and a desire for something else to happen; we often describe bored children as 'looking for trouble', and indeed they are, in a sense, genuinely looking for problems to solve. On the other hand, too much challenge results, in a variety of ways, in a retreat to safer ground.

A safe environment

A few decades ago, this regulating function was much in evidence in children's play outside the home – in streets and parks and playgrounds. Their play with friends outside the home was a crucial source of learning. Now the only secure alternative to playing out, where children can genuinely explore their world in safety, is the good early childhood education setting where exploration is encouraged. For most children, the world outside the home and away from 'important adults' is not generally a safe place to play. The congestion on our roads and the dimension of 'stranger-danger' are such that the challenges children are liable to meet outside the home without an adult may well be more devastating than manageable. As 'important people', we may have to recognise that allowing children to 'play out' represents an unacceptable risk.

This is a serious situation in terms of children's learning: they are being deprived of one of the main ways of learning about themselves, each other and their world. Increasingly, doors and windows are closing on children's opportunities for safe challenging play with other children. Neighbourhoods are not safe, and nursery education is not universally available to those children who need it. In recognising the consequences of this situation, we need to look carefully not only at what has been lost, but also at what is taking the place of this sort of play. It is profoundly worrying that, for many children, current alternatives may be limited to solitary play in the home and often to long hours in front of the television. These alternatives do not contain the learning experiences that children need for a rich childhood and for their normal development. It should surely be part of the social policy of national and local government to ensure that all children have the opportunities they need for safe play.

– PIPES AND GUTTERS –

❜ Now Lily's at nursery every morning, I don't see her so much; but the other day Mum said she thought they might like an extra pair of hands there sometimes, and would I like to go and help once a week? I think she really wants to go herself, but she can't just now, so I'm going instead. Sometimes there's lots to do, and I'm too busy to see what Lily's up too, but I can usually watch her for some of the time.

It was a lovely day last week when I went, and the best thing was the sand pit in the garden. They had lots of pipes and gutters in the sand; some of the children wanted *a water-run, and they'd worked out with the teacher how you could fit the pipes together and balance the top bit on a tower of milk crates. They've got a tap on the wall near the sand pit where the children can fill up their buckets, and the water they fetched went down all the pipes and into the big bucket at the bottom. Lily had a great time standing on a milk-crate and pouring her bucket of water into the top bit. After she'd done it, she scrambled down as fast as she could and rushed to see if the water was going into the bucket. Sometimes it fell out of a hole half-way down, and then she had to try and mend it. It always took a bit of thinking out, and sometimes it didn't work the first time and she had to try something else.*

Once she couldn't manage to make the corner bit stay on the pipe, and I thought she was going to make a big fuss, but the teacher helped her just in time. I thought the teacher was great, the way she knew exactly when Lily was nearly giving up. Then she just helped Lily enough so she could carry on.

When Lily tried to explain about the pipes and gutters to her dad, he said he didn't know what she meant, and couldn't she draw a picture to show him? She really wanted him to know about the pipes and she took ages drawing a plan of just how she remembered them. We all thought the plan was so good that she took it to show her teacher the next day; and she thought it was so good that she put it up in a special place on the wall so everyone could see it. Lily felt really proud of herself then. **'**

Some learning skills come naturally; these include exploring, questioning, experimenting and learning from mistakes

---

Exploratory learning

Babies are seeking creatures. They watch and listen and touch and smell and taste, working away at finding out. They are struggling for knowledge and control. As they grow in competence, their need to explore and control becomes increasingly demanding for us adults. Our efforts to contain this need result in much frustration for all concerned. Of course, much of the exploring must be contained for safety's sake, but the outcome may be, at least partially, to limit the child's development.

Isaacs (1954, p. 9) referred to the way in which children actively explore in order to solve their problems:

We have only to watch this play with a discerning eye, and to listen to his comments and questions, in order to realise how his mind is beset with problems of one sort or another – problems of skill, problems of seeing and understanding, problems of feeling and behaviour . . . He is always, in his own mind, concerned with watching and trying to understand and to deal with things and people, the objects in the world out-side him, which he so much needs to master and to comprehend.

This consciousness of problems to be solved and the drive to tackle them is, Isaacs said, the key to children's mental development. It unlocks the meaning of their behaviour.

Lily's efforts in the sandpit with the pipes and gutters were about investigating and controlling those objects. She was trying out ways of doing what she wanted, discovering new strategies and discarding old ones. She talked to the teacher while she was doing it, asking questions and trying new ideas. This exploring of the pipes and asking questions of the nearest adult was normal and natural for her. Another child might have been more reticent, but reticence comes when children are suppressing their exploring instincts.

Most 'important people' have a general idea of how they want their children to be and what they want them to know. If little progress is made with these aims, we have a tendency to say that a child is not learning. It can be challenging, but also useful, to realise that young children are inevitably and continuously learning; they do not remain blank until they can take in what we want them to know, but, like sponges, they constantly absorb an amazing amount of knowledge and understanding. They do not discriminate between what we want them to know and what we do not; they learn about all sorts of things that come their way. Smith (1978, p. 8) makes the point:

Children spend the first years of life solving problems all the time. Probably more learning takes place in the first two years than in any similar period thereafter. Children are born learning; if there is nothing to learn, they are bored, and their attention is distracted elsewhere. We do not have to train children to learn, or even account for their learning: we have to avoid interfering with it.

When a child does not seem to have learned what we hoped, instead of thinking that nothing was learned, it can be instructive to wonder what *was* learned instead. We may expect that a day in school will result in a greater understanding about, for instance, number concepts; yet the increase in understanding may be more related to problems of feeling and behaviour. An outing to the wildlife park will surely result in greater knowledge of the habits of monkeys, but the real lesson in life may turn out to be the use and misuse of public services, such as buses and lavatories. It may seem that a child has learned absolutely nothing from an experience such as an expedition to the supermarket; but much may actually have been learned or confirmed about adult expectations of behaviour in public, and individual levels of tolerance. It is not so much a question of *whether* children are learning, as *what* they are learning.

Children learn actively from their 'important people' and from the situations in which they find themselves. This is a challenging thought: what *are* they learning from living with us?

– BEING GOOD –

❛ There's a little girl in Lily's group called Amy. She's interested in what the others are all doing and she spends lots of time watching them, but she can't seem to join in. She seems to be really stuck. At first, I thought it was just because she wasn't used to being at nursery and maybe she felt a bit scared of doing anything in case she got it wrong. Some children seem to think everything's got to be right first time – they think there's only going to be one right way to do everything and they want you to tell them what it is. But then they don't have the fun of trying things out or the satisfaction of sorting something out for themselves.

Amy's mum really looks after her. When she brings her in the morning, she makes sure she's got everything she needs and she gives her a great big hug and tells her to be good. Amy really wants to please her mum and the teacher. Maybe that's why she doesn't try things out, or ask about things. Maybe she thinks if you make a mistake or don't know about something, it's not being good.

Yesterday, the teacher had mixed up some stuff for the children to play with and it was really messy. She told me that the children always love the way it looks different from how it feels, and they a learn a lot of early maths and science from playing with it. It's made of mixed-up cornflour and water and it looks all wet and sloppy but when you touch it, it feels dry. Lily thought it was wonderful – she spent ages scraping it up with her fingers and pouring it into little measuring pots and pretending things about it. All the time she was talking with the teacher about what she was doing, and so were the others. Amy stood behind the teacher and watched. But she wouldn't join in, so she never found out what the messy stuff felt like and how it pours into other things – and she missed a lot of fun.

After a while, the teacher left those children to get on by themselves and went to help some other children cook some little carrot cakes; she said she'd better keep an eye on them because you have to do cooking right if you want to eat it. Amy went too. I stayed to keep an eye on the cornflour, so I didn't see what happened next, but I heard the teacher telling Amy's mum that Amy had helped to make the cakes, so she must have felt all right about cooking. I wonder why she could do that, but not mess about with cornflour? ❜

In order to be 'socially acceptable', children often learn to behave in ways that inhibit learning

---

Adult expectations

If they are to thrive, babies and young children need their 'important people's' acceptance. The way in which they learn to be acceptable has been described earlier:

initially, the interaction between the mother and baby sets the scene, and this is developed further by other important people in the family, and gradually outside the family, too. Babies and young children learn which of their actions give particular pleasure, and lead to warm acceptance by their important people. Clearly, every important person will be unique in their values, but children learn that certain characteristics are particularly acceptable to parents and to teachers (Drummond, 1993, pp. 9–11).

Most children know that being acceptable generally involves obedience. When asked the question, 'When are your parents pleased with you?' (Roberts, 1993, p. 58), one child stated with clarity the principle that many others struggled in various ways to express. He said, 'You have to do what they say.' As soon as 'being good' was seen to be the issue, the discussion flowed. By the time they are three or four, children seem to be quite ready to identify what it means to be good. Although there may be disagreements between them about what is good and what is not, each child reckoned he or she had the answers; after all, they need to know. It is interesting that many of the answers seemed to be the result of *watching* what happens to others, rather than, for instance, remembering instructions. There seemed to be general agreement, amongst both children and adults, that being good means being obedient, especially when outside the home.

It requires considerable mental balance – which even many adults fail to attain – to be appropriately obedient *and* to ask questions. Is it realistic to expect children to do this? Does a four-year-old know when to conform and when to explore? Is it reasonable to expect young children to experiment and learn from mistakes at the same time as trying to be 'good'?

It may be that the situation is not as stark as this at home, but there can be little doubt that, outside the home, these are real questions for children, and therefore real questions for parents, teachers and others. To safeguard their perception of themselves as exploratory learners, they need their entitlement: enough freedom to explore their world.

8

Adults supporting learning

– TOO MUCH FOR TERRY –

❛ There was lots going on at the nursery when we went this week. I don't know how the teacher keeps an eye on it all. There were two students there a bit older than me, and they had to do something with the children and then write about it. I'd heard the teacher talking to them about it last week. She told them it wasn't enough to think about what the children needed to know and how they were going to teach them; they needed to watch the children more before they decided what to do. She said that if they chose something to do that wasn't connected with what the children know a bit about already the children wouldn't be able to make sense of it. The best way to find out what young children know about and what they're interested in, is to watch them and listen to them, she said.

I decided I would do a bit of watching and listening myself, when I wasn't doing things they asked me to do. It was a real eye-opener. There's a boy called Terry who never plays with the other children. When he first came to nursery his mum stayed with him for weeks and weeks because he didn't feel safe. Now he feels safe with his teacher and he even goes off and plays on his own sometimes, but not with the others. Anyway, yesterday I watched him.

He spent a long time sticking lots of those cardboard rolls that you get in the middle of cling film onto the top of a cereal box. He was really careful about it, and when he'd done about five in a row, he left the model on the bench – I don't know what it was supposed to be – and went off outside. Then Jessica came along and started cutting up bits of paper with what the children call the jiggy-jaggy scissors; they cut sort of teeth shapes. She said she was making a crocodile. Then she saw Terry's model on the table and she said, 'This can be my crocodile,' and she stuck the teeth onto the end of the box. There was an amazing collection of wood sticks and things in a box for making models with, and one of the mums asked Jessica why she didn't make her crocodile a cage? She said crocodiles are really dangerous, and we wouldn't want this one getting out, would we?

Jessica loved it. She was just putting the crocodile into the cage, when Terry came back. He watched her without saying anything. Then he saw me watching, and he came over and said, 'That's mine'. Jessica was so keen on her game with it that I asked him if she could borrow it for a bit longer. I said she'd made it into a crocodile and that she'd give it back to him very soon. He looked at me gloomily, then he looked at her playing with his model and then he turned round and went back into the garden. At first I thought that meant it was OK, but it wasn't. It was only because I caught sight of his face as he went through the door that I realised he was just beginning to cry.

It took ages to sort it out. First of all, Terry was so upset that he could only cry and not talk about it. Then he said he didn't want his model to be a crocodile. I asked why he didn't say that before and I tried to say that he should tell people what he wants and doesn't want, but I don't think he was listening; it was all too much. I knew we'd have to get the crocodile back from Jessica and take its teeth off, and I thought there'd be even more of a fuss about that, from her. I said to her that Terry was really upset, that we'd have to give his model back and that she could start again and make one all for herself. But she didn't mind at all; she looked at him carefully and then she just said 'OK, he can have it,' quite cheerfully and went off to do something else.

The teacher says Terry didn't get a chance to play with other children of his age much before he came to nursery and that Jessica's got a twin brother, so she's had more practice. She says Terry's getting better all the time, though. Perhaps that's why he didn't stand up for himself and why Jessica could manage without a fuss.

The students had a disappointment, though. They only come once a week, so this was their special day. They'd noticed last week that the children were interested in painting and mixing colours, so they decided to see if the children would be interested in doing a big green picture with just blue and yellow paint. The trouble was, they forgot to check with the teacher, so they didn't know the children often do that sort of thing and had done a big picture about mixing colours only two days before. They'd got it all ready at college, so when they got to nursery it was too late to change. It was a pity because nobody wanted to do it. When I showed Lily what the students had got ready she said, 'Done it,' and went off to play with Michael. In the end, they found a little group of girls who always like making things, but even they didn't stay very long or want to talk about it much, because it was nothing new or different.

The teacher said they were quite right to choose something like that, really, but that it needed to have something slightly different and special about it, otherwise the children wouldn't learn anything. **❯**

Learning involves struggle and adjustment. Too much struggle is overwhelming. Too little struggle means no adjustment

Levels of challenge

Children learn in situations which are neither undemanding nor overwhelming. We can use what we know about the process of learning to help children to build on what they already know, giving them opportunities to struggle, practise and play. This works best when we can incorporate security and enthusiasm into the child's learning. To do this, we need to know not only how to help them feel safe, but also about their previous knowledge, their particular interests and their individual patterns of learning.

It is a process of matching children's existing knowledge, understanding and forms of thought with curriculum content (Nutbrown, 1994, pp. 61–113). If we recognise the importance of knowing about children in order to help them with their learning, it is worth thinking about how we come to know them. We can use two approaches simultaneously: learning what we can about child development and children's learning generally, and learning what we can about each individual child (Bartholomew and Bruce, 1993).

Partnership between parents and staff

When it comes to getting to know individual children, their most important people – usually their parents – are the experts. The adults who live with and care for a child day after day, night after night, will have an accumulation of knowledge and understanding about that child which teachers can never hope to match (Whalley, 1994, pp. 61–2).

Staff in early childhood education settings and in primary schools may have learned a good deal about child development in their training and will have a body of experience to support their theoretical knowledge (Lally, 1991, pp. 94–6). Child development is about all aspects of a child's development: emotional, social and cognitive, as well as physical. It is only after a certain amount of training and experience that it becomes possible to differentiate between the 'normal' and the 'special' in children's behaviour and development. Staff with a wide range of experience, together with theoretical knowledge of 'normality', are able to recognise reliably what is 'normal' and what is 'special'.

Parents know best what is normal behaviour for their own children and what signals illness or upset. They can gain a great deal from books, papers and articles, too, but such reading usually applies to a *range* of real-life children, and what is 'normal' for one child may not be for another. Staff are therefore able to help parents check their perceptions of their children in the wider context. Another strategy that parents can, and often do, use is to watch other people's children and to make comparisons. This can be very useful as a means of identifying interests and patterns of learning; it works well when used as a way of focusing on what children *can* do. Much less useful is when comparisons are made unfavourably with other children, without taking developmental factors into account. Often this results in too high expectations, which most children find overwhelming.

We can make our knowledge and understanding work for children by developing alliances between parents and staff. These alliances are based on combining parents' knowledge of the child as an individual and staff knowledge of child development and children's learning in general. This is best done right from the beginning, from the first time a child enters a new learning environment away from the home. With an expectation of partnership on both sides, and with an attitude of give-and-take, parents and staff can use each other's knowledge and understanding to support the child's learning (Whalley, 1994, pp. 13–18). This is the bedrock of real home-school partnership.

Observing children

How do we get to know children? Using our eyes and ears seems an obvious and simple answer. But watching and listening to children is indeed of the utmost importance (Hurst, in Moyles, 1994, pp. 173–88). Often, however, we are under such pressure to get things done that stopping to watch and listen is much harder than it sounds. Parents of older children usually wish they had spent more time watching and listening to their young children, and members of staff frequently wish they had more time for observation of individual children.

Grandparents who are fortunate enough to have close contact with their grandchildren without the burden of round-the-clock care say that among the greatest pleasures are the opportunities to watch and listen. The fact that they are able to do that may account for the very special, close relationships that often develop between children and their grandparents.

The problem is not only one of time. So many of us, wholly understandably, do not fully realise the value and the need for watching and listening to children with detailed care and attention. The trouble is that we are often unaware of the gaps in our knowledge, and our understanding will always be partial. But nevertheless five or ten minutes of an adult's absolutely undivided attention on one child can be amazingly clarifying. There are also numerous occasions during the day at home and at school when the actions, feelings and talk of children may be seen or heard with attention, and accepted, by adults; or alternatively may pass unnoticed.

Careful watching involves an eye for detail and the exercise of curiosity. A great deal can be learned, particularly about feelings and attitudes, simply from watching children's body language when they are with each other or with other adults.

Watching carefully over a period of time enables an adult to gain insights into *why* children behave as they do and what particular events cause certain reactions.

How useful to discover that Lily concentrates particularly well at nursery on days when she has been able to say goodbye to Mum in a thorough and unhurried way, and to notice that Joe only does that sudden loud screaming that they couldn't understand when Mum *sits down* to talk to someone else. How reassuring and comforting for Lily when her 'important people' realise that saying goodbye properly really matters to her and do so accordingly; and how soothing for Joe to find that when Mum sits down to talk to people, she scoops him onto her lap so that he feels part of the conversation and can get down and go off to play when he wants to.

In particular, listening carefully to what children say and talking with them 'conversationally' rather than 'instructionally' is a revealing and rewarding process. Also – although it may sound like eavesdropping – the conversations that children have with each other or with another adult can be just as instructive as the conversations we have with them ourselves. Whether or not this is an invasion of their privacy may depend on *why* we watch and listen; occasionally to do so genuinely in order to understand children better, and thereby to support and care for them more appropriately, seems entirely valid.

The quality and usefulness of observations in early childhood education settings can depend on the ways in which they are recorded and used. A variety of possibilities can be considered (Bartholomew and Bruce, 1993, pp. 25–68). Watching and listening to children really carefully means that new experiences can be planned to connect with their existing knowledge and understanding. We know that this way of supporting and extending children's learning matches the learning process. It ensures that we do not waste precious time providing experiences at an inappropriate level. In addition, children's 'important people' are more likely to have *realistically* high expectations of them. This means that children are more liable to find themselves in situations which are just right for optimal learning: neither overwhelming nor lacking in challenge.

Behind the stereotypes

Some children who find life overwhelming are thought to be shy, anxious or even lazy. These children cannot seem to get on with things in the way that other children do. They watch a lot, hovering on the edge of other children's activities, either avoiding contact with adults or heavily dependent on them. Sometimes they seem to be oblivious to things around them and sometimes they will only play with a very few familiar things, unwilling to risk anything new.

Something is holding these children back from living their lives to the full. Often that something is an overload in their lives, of things that they cannot make sense of, or even begin to understand. They are incapacitated by too much struggling with the incomprehensible; nor do they have sufficient relevant and assimilated experiences to combine with new knowledge and understanding.

The trouble with verdicts like 'shy', 'anxious' and 'lazy' is that they describe a child's state without necessarily looking for causes. However, a 'shy' child may be affected by the sheer number of unknown people in his or her environment. An 'anxious' child may be struggling with an excessive amount of uncertainty. A 'lazy' child may be unable to respond to the level of expectation that he or she perceives is being demanded. Children who appear to fit these descriptions may, in fact, feel overwhelmed; asking ourselves the questions 'Overwhelmed by what?' and 'How can the pressure be eased?' may be more helpful than our usual responses to these characteristics.

– JOE AT NURSERY –

❝ Mum had a work problem this week and couldn't be with Joe in the mornings.

Usually on Lily's nursery day, I take Lily and Mum stays at home with Joe. Mum said did I think I could manage to look after Joe for her by taking him to nursery? Or would it be better if I stayed at home just this week? In the end, we decided that he'd probably like it at nursery and that, now Lily's really settled down, I could keep an eye on him as well as being a bit of a help to the other children sometimes.

Well, it was the hardest morning ever! Once or twice I thought we were going to have to give up and go home. Joe absolutely loved it, but he couldn't wait to find out about everything, so as soon as he'd started doing something, he was off to the next thing. The teacher was really understanding; as soon as she saw Joe, she said she was really glad he'd come, but that I'd better spend the morning keeping an eye on him and not try to do anything else. She looked pleased when I said he didn't put things in his mouth all the time any more.

Once, I stopped for a minute to help Michael do up his shoes. I thought Joe was happy standing on a box pouring water into a giant bottle in the water tray, but when I'd done the shoe, Joe had vanished. In the end, I found him on the other side of the garden at the top of the scramble net. He was really pleased to be at the top, but he couldn't get down because his shoe was caught in the rope. As soon as I'd lifted him down, he wanted to climb up again, but that time he didn't get stuck.

It was very muddy in the garden from all the rain, and there was a huge puddle that the children were riding the bikes through, lifting up their feet so they didn't get wet. Of course, Joe didn't know how to lift his feet up, so we had to go and find a dry pair of trousers in the cupboard. Then he wanted to do the fingerpainting in the workshop. I don't know how he managed to get the paint up past his elbows and into his hair. The teacher laughed and said he'd done a really thorough job. She said she liked seeing children having a go at things.

Joe didn't learn from the puddle mistake, though, although he did learn that it was fun to go whizzing through puddles. He loved it so much that he had another go when I thought he was playing in the sand pit, and got wet all over again! In the end, I decided that it wouldn't hurt him to be a bit wet as it wasn't cold, so I left him. It was just as well I hadn't changed him again – next he found the little, blue paddling pool *full of earth and water; and had a wonderful time making mud pies. When it was time to go home he looked like a mud pie himself, and I spent all afternoon washing muddy clothes while he had his sleep. As soon as he woke up, he wanted to go again!*

Some learning skills come naturally; these include exploring, questioning, experimenting and learning from mistakes

---

Encouraging exploratory learning

The essentially exploring nature of young children is recognised as being crucial to their learning (Isaacs, 1954, pp. 20–1). However, living with exploring children of this age is a major challenge. There is a constant need to strike the right balance between challenge and safety. Children need to be encouraged to explore, discover and learn from their mistakes. They need to find out about their world and about the consequences of their actions in it. But, at the same time, they must be protected from physical danger and from extreme distress.

It is not easy to get this balance right. Adequate safety is easy to remember, with the threat of dangerous consequences; children are more secure when clear boundaries have been defined about when, where and how they can explore, question and try things out. Allowing young children enough exploration may be harder, especially as it can sometimes result in a certain amount of inconvenience. It can be helpful to remember that questioning and exploring are *natural* activities for young children.

There are three important things that we can do to meet children's needs for exploratory activity: ensure they have enough *time* to explore, enough *space* and enough *attention* (Singer, 1990, pp. 153–75). Children's lives all too often tend to reflect the pace of their parents', and for some, this means a busy life. Exploring is not just about rushing around doing things; it is also about watching, listening and reflecting. Sometimes, when children appear to be doing nothing, they are actually working very hard at the process of exploration.

As well as time, children need enough space: to move around, to make choices, to allow a measure of independence from the nearest adult. This can be difficult to achieve in crowded families and small play areas and classrooms. Where 'playing out' is no longer safe, the provision of play areas that *are* safe for children should be high on the agenda of new building developments and of communities able to improve their facilities.

The third dimension that we can give children is our attention – to deal with questions honestly, to make time to find out about their interests and intentions, and to help them think confidently about their successes and mistakes. They need our attention in listening, valuing, questioning and encouraging; and they need our commitment to provide a variety of interesting, relevant experiences in which they can be actively involved.

Setting examples for children

A question which crops up time and again is: what sort of role models are we for children? Do *we* explore, experiment and learn from mistakes? It is hard to over-estimate the influence we have in this respect. Children need our acceptance and approval, and they try to be like their 'important adults'. If we always have the right answer, children get the idea that it is never all right not to know. If we never try something out unless we know that it will work, our implicit message to them is, 'Don't risk it'. If our attitude to failure is to hide and deny it, how will they learn to accept and think about their mistakes in order to do things better next time?

We all know children and adults – maybe sometimes ourselves among them – who rarely go looking for something new, who always have an answer, who never risk making a mistake. How did we get like that? What altered our naturally exploring, experimenting early childhood characters? Pressure to 'get things right' is increasing. Both in homes and outside, there is more awareness of the very real dangers and consequences of doing things wrong; and in schools, there is greater pressure for assessment of skills, knowledge and understanding, rather than of effort and progress.

Accurate assessment is, of course, crucial for high-quality teaching; good teachers have always been aware of this and welcome opportunities to sharpen their focus. But we need to be very vigilant about the messages we give to children about 'right' and 'wrong' answers if we are to continue to nurture their natural learning skills (Drummond, 1993, p. 95). The pressures to 'get it right' are the very pressures that threaten to impair children's ability to think creatively and learn effectively. In all areas of their lives, the ability to remember facts will indeed be useful; but the habit of trying out solutions, the knowledge that mistakes are a normal part of learning, and the attitude that accepts and uses them positively, will be crucial.

Of course, there are occasions when we need to get things as 'right' as possible: for instance, in examinations, important public events, celebrations for other people. But these are 'one-offs'. Day by day, together with consistent effort, what counts in successful learning are habits of reasonably safe exploration, experimentation and reflection. Accepting and using both success *and* failure is what serves learning best.

– PRETEND PAINTING –

❝ There's a big change in Amy at the nursery these days. When she first came, she didn't do anything much, especially not on her own or with the other children. She always had to be with the teacher and she only liked making things to take home. She didn't play with anything else much or do any exploring. She was kind of opposite to how Joe was that day he came to nursery.

I think the teacher decided it was time to persuade Amy that it was OK to go and try things out and make a few mistakes, and even make a bit of a mess sometimes – so long as she helps to clear it up. Maybe she needed to persuade Amy's mum, too. One day the teacher asked Amy's mum if she could drop in for a cup of tea on the way home, and her mum was really pleased. She said Amy could show her her favourite toys, and that she would buy a special cake, but the teacher said she was on a diet!

Anyway, ever since then Amy has been different. Yesterday was really good. Michael and Lily had made a camp by hanging an old sheet over two tables so they could get underneath; but they wanted one side of the sheet to lift up higher so their camp could have a sort of outside bit. Once before the teacher had made a camp like that by tying bits of string to two corners of the sheet and fixing the string to hooks on the wall. Amy must have seen her because she went off and asked for string, and she got the scissors and she did just the same thing. The others thought it was really clever of her and I did too; I had to help her with the tying, but I'd forgotten about doing that until she remembered.

Then I was even more surprised, because soon after that, she went and did pretend painting with Lily and Michael. They do it sometimes when it's hot. They had the great big paint brushes and buckets of water and they were pretending to be decorators coming to paint the play house in the den. I think Michael must have seen a real painter at home or somewhere, because he kept stirring up the water and sloshing it on with the real up-and-down strokes. It all got a bit wild, and they were giggling and getting wet, and in a minute I thought they'd be painting each other so I said, 'Isn't it time for your tea break?' And Amy said to Michael, 'Do you take sugar?' Then she pretended it was her house and went to make the tea; and Lily pretended to be the boss and told Michael his painting wasn't very good and he'd have to do it again.

Amy came back with pretend tea on a tray from the home corner and they decided to have it in the camp – and all that time Amy didn't seem to worry about making a mess or fetching things they needed. Perhaps she's changed her mind about what nursery's for. **9**

In order to be 'socially acceptable', children often learn to behave in ways that inhibit learning

Factors inhibiting learning

Our dilemma is that we all want our children to be successful learners; but we also want to help them to fit into families and society, which seems to mean less exploring and more restraint about their feelings. We may feel, particularly outside the home, that the two traits of exploring and of expressing negative feelings as well as positive ones are indeed unacceptable. If so, must we then 'give up' on those two crucial aspects of children's learning?

It can be argued that children are liable to be cognitively disabled without the development of exploratory learning skills. It can also be argued that giving up on children's ability to acknowledge and express – and thereby begin to resolve – feelings of pain, fear and anger also carries major penalties. If we fail to acknowledge a child's need to resolve these feelings, then the child may consequently lack determination, clarity and confidence; and yet these characteristics – so vital in many aspects of living – are also needed in order to develop as an exploratory learner.

Studies which focus on this dilemma are reported by Sylva (in Ball, 1994, pp. 91–4). Children are categorised as 'mastery' children and 'helpless' children. Here is her summary of the results:

- *Helpless children avoid challenge and give up easily, whereas mastery-oriented children persist in the face of obstacles and seek new, challenging experiences;*
- *Helpless children report negative feelings and views of themselves when they meet obstacles, while 'mastery' children have positive views of their competence and enjoy challenges;*
- *The style of 'helpless'- or 'mastery'-oriented behaviour is not related to intelligence; rather, it is a personality characteristic, a way of viewing oneself and one's capacity to be effective with things and people.*

This issue about 'mastery' and 'helplessness' is an important factor. We know that children are naturally active, learning best by exploring, questioning and experimenting. We also know that the most sociable and successful children are those who manage to *combine* their exploratory learning with an awareness of others. However, in the previously mentioned study about the development of children's self-perception (Roberts, 1993, p. 64), it emerged that a majority of the children in the study did not see themselves as exploratory, but preferred to think of themselves as receptive.

Two groups were particularly significant, where the children were almost unanimous in seeing themselves as receptive. One was a group from a particularly disadvantaged housing estate; the other was a group whose parents had very high expectations of their children. It appeared that, at four years old, both these groups of children had already learned – for very different reasons – that to risk getting things wrong was too dangerous. They could no longer imagine themselves behaving in a 'normal' exploratory way. Here again, we are seeing what happens when children feel overwhelmed. There may not be a great deal we can do about the causes, but what we can do is recognise children's feelings and responses, and make sure that they do have the opportunities for safe exploration that they need.

Staff and parents need to work together to clarify for children the expectations of adults in those special places where children go to learn. Children need to know that schools are unique places, different from home, but also different from being 'out' in the general sense. They need to know that in schools they are expected to take a measure of ownership and a measure of responsibility; that exploring and expressing feelings is both necessary and desirable; that it is safe to be themselves as deeply and widely as they can; and that they will learn about their place as an individual within a group.

Obviously it is important that children do learn to behave in ways that are socially acceptable. In addition, schools should be established as places where it is safe to explore and experiment, where making mistakes is seen as normal and useful, and where questions and discussions are encouraged. Many would argue that this happens already; undoubtedly it is their *intention* that children should feel this way about school. However, we do need to question children's actual perceptions about appropriate learning behaviour at school (Pascal, 1990, p. 32).

Places where they go to learn will never, for most children, feel as safe as home. But it is our job to make sure that children know that schools are *relatively* safe places. An effective way to work on this re-definition of schools is by setting our example. If we, as staff and parents, are willing to value ourselves and each other, to try things out when we are uncertain of the result, to celebrate successes and mistakes and be honest about our feelings, children are likely to follow our lead. Changing the habits of a lifetime may be hard, but the results for children would be worth the struggle.

POSTSCRIPT TO PART 4: LINKING WITH LEARNING

Living or working with young children?
Questions to think about . . .

> **Learning involves struggle and adjustment. Too much struggle is overwhelming. Too little struggle means no adjustment**

1. How do we form our expectations of children? What can we do to try and make sure they are appropriate?

> **Some learning skills come naturally; these include exploring, questioning, experimenting and learning from mistakes**

2. How good are we at modelling learning skills for children? Do they see us exploring, questioning, experimenting and learning from mistakes?

> **In order to be 'socially acceptable', children often learn to behave in ways that inhibit learning**

3. What social behaviours do we expect of children? And what learning behaviours? Are these expectations compatible, or do children sometimes receive mixed messages from their 'important adults' about what is expected of them?

RECOMMENDED FURTHER READING

For sharing with children . . .

Waddell, M. & Firth, B. (1999), *Well Done, Little Bear***, London, Walker Books**
Another lovely book from Martin Waddell, this one is about a young learner, Little Bear, exploring and learning from mistakes. The loving adult, Big Bear, encourages, supports, rescues, comforts, allows herself (or himself, it could very satisfactorily be either) to be led, and finally talks with Little Bear about the adventure. This is a satisfying picture of the parent-child relationship, offering a security that comforts adult and child alike.

For a good read . . .

Abbott, L. & Nutbrown, C. (2001), *Experiencing Reggio Emilia: implications for pre-school provision***, Buckingham, Open University Press**
Loris Malaguzzi's dedication to this book refers to children as 'rich in potential, powerful, competent and most of all connected to adults and other children'. A study visit to Reggio Emilia by this group of highly experienced early childhood educators reflects their impressions and experiences, and has generated a collection of contributions to this book on the 'Reggio approach' which are thoughtful, reflective, instructive and challenging.

For reference . . .

Lee, V. & Das Gupta, P. (1995), *Children's Cognitive and Language Development***, Buckingham, Open University Press**
Another in the OUP series mentioned in Part 2's Postscript, this is also comprehensive and reliable, with activities that encourage the reader's active involvement. It focuses on cognition, with contributions on theories of cognitive and language development, models of memory development, categorisation, concepts and reasoning, the development of intelligence, mathematical and scientific thinking, and development in drawing and reading.

PART 5

REAL SELF-ESTEEM

9

Children's successful learning

– LILY AND JOE'S PICNIC –

❝ Lily's just got a new buggy for her two dolls, and there's a place underneath where she can put things like pretend picnics for them. She used to play picnics with the little old truck that was for the wooden bricks, but now she's given that to Joe. He's really pleased – he puts things in it and wheels it about; but he's having to learn how to steer it. It's easier for him to pull it than push it, but he doesn't like doing that because then he isn't doing it like Lily.

Lily and Joe had a great game outside today. Lily decided to take her dolls for a walk, and Joe trailed along after. He made a fuss at first, because there wasn't anything in his truck, but Lily dropped in some old bits of Duplo that were on the floor, and then he was quite happy. I don't think he realised that the game was about dolls; he just wanted to wheel his truck with something in it.

When they came to the big tree, Lily propped up the dolls on the grass by the trunk and emptied out all the bits and pieces from underneath the buggy. Joe just watched. Lily looked at the dolls thoughtfully. Then she said they were hungry and she'd have to go to the shop because there wasn't enough to eat. 'They'd better have a sleep,' she said, busily laying them down and tucking the little blanket over them. 'Stay there, children – I won't be long!' she said in her grown-up voice. Then she grabbed the handle of the buggy and went off back towards the house. 'I have to make a shopping list,' she muttered to herself as she passed me.

Joe tried to get the truck to go forwards like Lily did with the buggy, but the wheels wouldn't work because they were covered in mud. I showed him how to scrape the mud off one wheel with a stick; and then I said he could do the rest. He wanted me to do it for him, but I said I'd watch, and if he really couldn't do it, I'd help him. So he had a go at the others; and he did it quite well, so after that the truck worked. He was really pleased with himself

Lily had found an old list of Mum's and added some writing of her own. 'This says "special cheese and Dinocrackers and apples",' she told me and Joe. Dinocrackers are her favourites. I asked her where the shop was. 'There,' she said, pointing to the store-cupboard that Mum was clearing out.

'I hope you've got some money, then!' Mum said. She was just coming out with a load of old boxes and packets.

'We need a picnic,' said Lily firmly, holding out the list. Joe edged up a bit nearer. Mum said they could have some of the boxes she was throwing away, for pretending, and they'd need something to put them in. She said Lily would have to make sure that Joe didn't eat anything because it was all a bit old and he might get a tummy-ache.

They spent ages going backwards and forwards between the store-cupboard and the kitchen with empty and half-full boxes, bags, trays and baskets. After a bit, Joe got fed up with trailing backwards and forwards carrying things; he had a great time instead standing on the big tree root throwing all the empty boxes down into his truck. Then he found a cereal packet with some old cereal left in the bottom; and he was just putting a handful in his mouth when Lily spotted him. She hadn't forgotten what Mum had said, so with one hand she grabbed the box and with the other Joe's hand with the old cereal in it. Of course, there was a struggle, and Joe screamed and Lily shouted and Joe pulled her hair, all in half a minute.

When I'd dragged them apart, I said to Lily that she'd have to think of a clever way to stop Joe eating the old cereal, not just grab it off him. Joe looked as if he was going to start screaming again, so I sat him on my knee and told him Lily had something very special to tell him – and then we looked at Lily to see what she would say. Lily looked at Joe, and then she looked at the old box, and then she said, 'You can have some new cereal in a bowl if you like.' Then she pointed towards the house, and Joe got off my lap, and they went off to find it.

Lily got her dolls all sorted out in the end. She made them sit up and eat their picnic, and then she told them a long story about a magic rabbit that lived underneath the tree. I think it was the one that her dad told her last week; Joe thought it was really good at first, but after a bit he pushed off with his truck. When Mum saw the mess under the tree, she said she had sorted out all the boxes and things once and she wasn't going to do it all over again. She gave us a rubbish bag and said if I held it open, Lily could put all the boxes in, now the dolls had had their picnic. Lily really liked putting everything in the bag – she was so keen, I thought she might put the dolls in too, but then she said it was time they had a rest in their cots. She walked off towards the house dragging the rubbish bag behind her, with a couple of little blankets in the other hand, and the two dolls tucked carefully one under each arm. **9**

Children are encouraged to learn when someone knows what they especially want to do and can nearly manage, and helps them to manage it successfully

Learning and play

Encouraging and helping young children to learn must be one of the most fundamental of our tasks as 'important adults'. Three factors can be helpful here. First, we need to think about how young children go about learning; second, we need to identify the most effective things we can do to help them; and third, we need to understand ways in which realistic, high self-esteem can be achieved.

These are the main issues in these two chapters, and although the sections deal with various separate aspects for the sake of clarity, the issues are, in reality, all interwoven and interdependent. The whole picture is viewed through the perspective of the child's self-esteem, which is seen as the key to balanced development and learning.

Young children learn effectively in a number of ways. These include exploring, observing and listening, representing first-hand experiences in a variety of ways, and play involving a combination of ideas, feelings and relationships with the application of skills and competence. Playing and talking are, for young children, two principal means of bringing together a range of these activities (D.E.S., 1990, p. 11).

It is often said that children learn through play; there is, however, less agreement about exactly what is meant by play. Bruce (1991, p. 3) illuminates the debate about play by describing the two main categories of play theory as 'play versus work' theories and 'play as education' theories. 'Play versus work' theories define play negatively in terms of what it is not (e.g. not work). The 'play as education' strand, dealing with play as preparation for life, tends to see it as preconceived and dominated by adults, who, of course, know what life holds in store. There may, however, be particular concern about preparing for the future at the expense of meeting children's current needs.

It is the 'play as an integrating mechanism' model – referred to by Bruce as 'free-flow play' – that best enables the creative end result of previous struggle and practice. The characteristics of free-flow play as described by Bruce allow for the combination of ideas, feelings and relationships (intention) with the application of competence and technical prowess (knowledge and skill). When children (or adults) are using this combination of intention and knowledge and skill, they are playing – or working – creatively. It would be helpful if the word 'play' were only used to refer to this essentially creative process. At every level, from sensory-motor babyhood to the most abstract adult thought, it is new *combinations* of understanding from which new hypotheses are formed and new discoveries are made. This is when 'the penny drops', when the wonderful 'eureka' moments occur. Indeed, it could be said that children learn – by watching, listening, exploring and representing their experiences, gaining knowledge and understanding and developing skills – primarily in order to play. All these aspects of learning culminate in play.

It follows, therefore, that providing children with opportunities to play (creatively to use their own intentions, understanding, knowledge and competence) is ensuring learning at the point where it becomes fun. Children who can play at home and who have had the benefit of quality early childhood education settings are generally eager to learn, cheerfully responsive and full of curiosity. They thrive on a balance of exploration, developing knowledge and skills, together with any opportunities to experience the fundamental satisfaction of playing creatively.

For many children, however, such settings are not available. Donaldson (1978, p. 14) suggested that large numbers of children:

> . . . leave school with the bitter taste of defeat in them, not having mastered even moderately well those basic skills which society demands, much less having become people who rejoice in the exercise of creative intelligence.

It must be acknowledged that this is still liable to be true in the twenty-first century; and although the reasons are becoming ever more complex and inter-related, it can be strongly argued that one reason for this is a lack of recognition of the value of free-flow play beyond the Foundation Stage. As children grow older, time for play (in the creative sense), both in the classroom and at home, is usually curtailed. Many children who continue to learn do so for extrinsic reasons, such as reward systems, testing or the need for adult approval. Unfortunately, however, these reasons for learning seldom stand the test of time. Research into the benefits of early childhood education (Sylva, in Ball, 1994, pp. 84–94) has shown that the effects of well-assimilated skills, knowledge and understanding stay with children and positively affect their lives. Well-assimilated learning can be used in creative combinations bringing pleasure and the intrinsic motivation to learn more.

Supporting children's efforts

A crucially important idea in relation to encouraging and supporting children's learning is about identifying and focusing on what children can *nearly* do. This area of children's development is seen as distinct from the area of development on which we usually focus: what children can do on their own without help. In planning for children's learning, it has been our practice to measure children's knowledge, understanding and competence in order to determine at what level we may best help them. In the past, it has been generally assumed that anything a child needed help with did not count for assessment; in fact, to include in an assessment of a child's learning something that he or she needed help with felt like cheating. Currently we have begun to see the implications of the proposition (Vygotsky, 1978, p. 86) that, in planning to support children's learning, we should focus primarily on those things that children can *nearly* do on their own, rather than using as our starting points the things they can already do without help.

Clearly this proposition makes sense. Knowing the actual levels of development and achievement that children have reached is certainly important. But all children are not going to learn exactly the same things and in a standard order. Knowledge about what children have already learned tells us nothing at all about what children are *currently* engaged in learning. We will surely help children to learn more effectively by focusing on what they want and are trying to do and what they can begin to manage with a bit of help and encouragement from someone who is at least a few steps ahead.

In relation to finding out more about a child's ability, Vygotsky suggests that it is the rate at which a child can cover the ground between the level of doing something now with help and the level of doing it independently which tells us most about the child's current potential. The area between those two levels is the cutting edge of each child's learning – Vygotsky's name for it is 'the zone of proximal development'. How long will it take Joe to learn to find a stick and scrape the mud off the wheels of his truck without anyone suggesting it or helping him? Will Lily be able to use what she learned about managing Joe to handle a similar situation on her own tomorrow? or next week? or next year? The answers to these questions would tell us more about Joe and Lily's future ability to learn than would a couple of statements such as, 'Joe can scrape mud off wheels' or 'Lily can manage Joe'.

Helping children to help themselves

If we want to be really effective in helping children in their learning, we need to be thinking, day by day, about what it is that they are *trying* to do; and about what it is they *could* do, with a little help from us. This process of supporting children in their learning until they can manage on their own is sometimes referred to as 'scaffolding' learning (Bruner and Haste, 1987, pp. 21–2). Scaffolding, in the learning context, implies the use of talking and listening by an adult or more able child, in order to support the learners' efforts. So when Joe needed to make the truck work, he was supported by encouragement and offers of help if he needed it; and when Lily needed to sort out Joe, she was supported by the expectation that she would think of something appropriate and effective – which she did. The help that Lily received from Mum that morning made it easier for Lily to do things that she either wanted or needed to do: Mum supplied Lily with boxes for her game at the very point at which she needed them, and Mum suggested a way of clearing up that would appeal to Lily.

The idea of 'scaffolding' is akin to the ideas of 'holding' and 'containment' which were considered earlier in this book. Some of those practical suggestions, for instance about acceptance and role-modelling, apply here too. Thinking back to our own learning experiences (such as, for instance, our early days of living and working with children), how important was it to us to receive support? What was the most helpful kind of support we received from others with more experience, as we found our feet? Were we conscious of progressing from needing support to managing on our own? The answers to these questions may provide some insight into the implications of Vygotsky's ideas about ways to support children's learning.

– MOVING HOUSE –

❝ I saw Lily's new friend at nursery today. She's called Henna, and Lily has been talking about her all the week. When we got to nursery, Henna hadn't arrived yet, and the teacher asked Lily if she'd like to help get the things out of the shed in the garden; but Lily shook her head and waited by the door till Henna came.

I was really surprised when I saw Henna. I thought she was going to be sparkly and full of beans, the way Lily talked about her. But she was little and quiet. She smiled a huge smile when she saw Lily waiting for her, but she didn't say anything. She and her mum had come with Nerinda and Imran and their mums, and they were all busy talking together, so Lily and Henna went off into the playroom, to the home corner.

I had to go and help with the children in the paddling pool in the garden, so I didn't see them for a while. When I went back to the home corner to look for them, they'd gone – and so had nearly all the things in the home corner! It turned out that they were playing 'moving house' and they'd made another house just outside by the woodwork bench. There's a big table there, and the teacher had given them a blanket to put over it, and they'd made the new house inside.

It was quite crowded in there, but really neat. They had the little cooker, the cupboard, and all the cutlery and the pretend food. They had a blanket for a bed as well, and it was folded over so you could get inside. They even had the telephone! One of the mums told me that Lily had done most of the fetching and carrying, and Henna was the one who sorted things out. When the teacher said it was nearly time to clear up, I thought Lily would make an awful fuss, but she didn't; Henna was really organised, and they went backwards and forwards quite happily until it was all done.

When I told Lily's dad about it in the evening, he laughed and said Lily sounded like his mate who does a delivery job, and perhaps Lily will end up driving lorries too! And Mum said she'd rather Lily was more like Henna, then she'd be better at putting her toys back in the cupboard and shutting the door, instead of leaving them all over the house. ❞

Recognising and supporting the development of children's patterns of learning, or schemas, leads to high self-esteem

Children's patterns of learning (schemas)

Kant first wrote about the idea of schemas 250 years ago, calling it schematism (Walsh, in Wolff, 1968, pp. 71–87). Much later, Piaget (1953) illustrated schemas from the earliest co-ordinations right through to the symbolic co-ordinating of symbolic functioning. Comprehensive and clarifying work on schemas is to be found in Athey's book (1990), which describes the Froebel project study. Bruce (1991) and Nutbrown (1994) have written about schemas, showing how an awareness of them can be used to support and extend children's learning. Much work about schemas has been done by parents and staff together, particularly at Redford House Nursery (Bartholomew and Bruce, 1993) and at the Pen Green Centre for Families and Children Under Five (Whalley, 1994). The PEEP Project makes these ideas accessible to parents and carers in the PEEP 'Learning Together' series (PEEP, 2000), especially in the Summer section of 'Learning Together with Threes'.

The recognition and development of children's schemas – or patterns of learning – can be a key to effective ways of helping children to learn, and to raise their self-esteem. Schemas are, simply, patterns of repeatable behaviour in children. We have seen, for instance, a strong pattern in Lily's play in relation to moving things from one place to another. Lily's strong schema at the moment is about 'transporting'. Lily's friend Henna has a different pattern: her play shows that she loves covering things up and putting things into other things. Her schemas are enveloping and containing.

These patterns are likely to run through everything that Lily and Henna do at the moment. For instance, Lily loves being asked to serve out at tea-time, which involves transferring food from dish to plate; and she often takes her mattress off her bed and re-makes it on the other side of the room or even out on the landing. She loves board games like Lotto and Snakes and Ladders that involve moving counters horizontally and vertically, and her favourite treat is a journey of any sort.

Henna's play reflects different patterns. Her best toy as a toddler was a posting box, and her favourite game was when her mum put a cot sheet right over the top of her cot, and she had a cosy den inside. Henna spends long periods at the water tray filling up jugs and bottles, and when she gets a new toy, she's more likely to play with the box it came in than with the toy itself.

Lily's friend Dan is a 'trajectory' child. He loves running, jumping, throwing and kicking – in fact, anything involving lines and movement. Later on, unless his schemas change dramatically, he might well be especially interested in guns, bows and arrows and rockets; he loves the garden games at nursery, like 'hit the bottle', the punch bag, skittles, and the goal posts.

The construction sets, the train track, and glueing are favourite activities for Michael and Jessica. These two love joining things together, so they have a passion for string and Sellotape, laying wooden bricks end to end in a long line, and hanging up washing with clothes pegs. The schema these share is connection.

Amy is especially interested in circle games, roundabouts and things with wheels; she loves watching the clothes going round in the washing machine, and one week she was fascinated by the concrete mixer outside the nursery. Her schema is rotation.

Although children often show particular schemas in their play, not all children appear especially schematic. Some show one schema particularly strongly, and others show several at once. Sometimes one schema that has been particularly strong will seem to fade, possibly to be replaced by another.

Sometimes the results of young children's play seem particularly messy or destructive. Glue gets in the wrong place, contents of drawers and cupboards are transferred to other places, things are thrown, furniture is jumped on – or off! Some schemas, such as 'transporting' and 'trajectory' play, are often inconvenient, both at home and at school. An insight into the schematic compulsions at the heart of this sort of play can help us to provide for children's needs in a more manageable way. Doing this avoids much frustration for adults and gives considerable satisfaction to children. For instance, the provision of an old shopping basket and some empty boxes and tins will go a long way to prevent the apparently random redistribution of other, more precious, objects; and there is a wide range of alternatives, from instruction in the making of paper aeroplanes to the provision of an old mattress specially for bouncing, which will meet the needs of the 'trajectory' child, whose interests include throwing and jumping.

One of the most valuable aspects of providing for schematic activity is that, in doing so, we are recognising and valuing children's fundamental interests and needs. This is a powerful way of genuinely raising children's self-esteem. Instead of the likelihood of disapproval for playing in ways that seem normal and natural to them, we can make provision for children to play in the ways that they need to, safely and acceptably. In this way, we are letting children know that we accept how they are and what they want to do. In the warmth of approval, positive self-concept thrives.

– BUILDING A DEN –

❝ Last week there was a special day at the nursery when everyone went to help. It was a good thing that it was on my Saturday off, so I didn't miss it. They called it 'Gardening and Mending Day', and it was so that lots of things got mended and sorted out.

They'd started to plan it the week before, so I knew a bit about it already. First, they made a list of all the jobs that needed doing and the problems that needed sorting out.

I don't remember all of them, but it was things like mending the fence where the hole is and putting the wheels back on the cart. As well as mending things, they wanted to make some new things for the children in the garden, like a pulley in the tree, for hauling things up and down, and a washing line for hanging up dolls' clothes when the children have washed them. Another thing they wanted was a special place where the children could make dens and tents out of old sheets and bits of string, but without starting right from the beginning every time; so it needed some hooks in the right places and somewhere to store the string and sheets and things.

The list of things was on the notice board, so you could sign up for what you wanted to do. I really liked the sound of the place for dens, and I knew Lily would love it, too, so that's what I signed up for. They said that children could help too if they liked; or they could play so long as they kept out of the way

It was a lovely day, which was lucky because we had a picnic, and there wouldn't have been room for everyone inside if it had rained. Mum said it would be best if Joe stayed at home with her; she thought it would be easier for everyone, and she said she didn't want him getting covered in the red paint they were going to paint the home-corner with! On the way, Lily wanted to know what we were going to do, and I told her about sorting out how to make a den. I was right, she wanted to know all about how we could make it stay up. I said I didn't know, and that we'd have to think about that when we were doing it.

When we got there, it was really busy. Lily's friend Dan was there; his mum and dad were mending the trucks, and so was Imran's dad. The teacher gave me the things to make the den with and showed me where she wanted it. I told Lily I thought it would be great if she could help me, and the teacher said Lily was just the person to sort it out, so off we went. Dan and Imran came too; Dan said they could play in the den when we'd made it, and Lily said he'd have to help make it then.

The place was under the tree that the children climb in, near the swing. The teacher said we could use the little wooden climbing frame, if we wanted. She'd given us hooks, nappy pins, three old sheets, a ball of string and some clothes pegs. She also said that she thought there were a couple of tent poles in the shed, and they might be useful.

It was really good that the children helped, because they knew what they wanted; if it had been only me, I wouldn't have done it the same at all. First of all, we sat on the grass and talked about dens and what you want them for. Dan said they were for hiding, so they had to have a roof and be dark, and Lily said they had to have two doors, one for going in and one for getting out. Imran said they were for eating things in, and Lily said, 'And for milk'. Then Imran said baddies aren't allowed, and the others agreed. I asked who was a baddie, and they looked at each other a bit ashamed and didn't say anything. I know the teacher doesn't like them talking about baddies; once I heard her saying they use it as a way of keeping some children out of their games, and that's unkind to those children.

We talked about how big to make it and how to hold it up. They thought using the climbing frame would be best, but when we got it out, we found it wouldn't go under the lowest branch of the tree, so that was no good. Then they said we could hold it up with string, and so we tied one end to the branch – but there was nothing to hold up the other end. Lily thought we could just put it over another branch, but then she said the den wouldn't be big enough for their game. In the end, Dan remembered the tent poles, and we found them in the corner of the shed. Then we got on really well, because Dan's family goes camping, and he knows all about guy ropes and things, so he was the boss for that bit. There was a bit of a pause when we couldn't find any pegs for the ends of the string, but Imran said he'd seen them on the high-up shelf in the shed, and he was right.

After a long time, we got it all sorted out and it was really good. There was a way in where the brown sheet was, and a gap at the back for going out, and it was big enough for lots of children. We had two long bits of string to hold the sheets up, and both tent poles, and lots of tent pegs and clothes pegs. When the teacher saw it, she looked really pleased. She said if we thought it was just right, hadn't we better draw a plan so we could make it again whenever we liked? So Lily rushed off to get a big piece of paper and some pens, and we put stickers on the poles and pegs, so when we put them in a special bag, we would be able td find them again.

Lily's plan was just finished by picnic-time, and the teacher said it would be really useful; she stuck it up on the back of the shed door so everyone would know how to make the den from now on. After lunch, I went to help with the painting, but Lily, Dan and Imran played in the den right to the end when it was time to go home, and they really took turns and didn't wreck it in the end, like they do sometimes. After they'd put it all away I saw them standing in front of the plan, pointing at bits. They looked just like a gang of builders! **?**

Children learn well with a combination of appropriately high expectations and appropriately high self-esteem

About expectations

This statement can be taken to refer to children's own expectations of themselves or to the expectations of their 'important adults'. Children's own expectations are comparatively straightforward to consider, if one is also engaged in considering their self-concept, as the one will inform the other. If children's self-concept is appropriately positive, then, correspondingly, their self-expectation is likely to be appropriately high.

The question of adults' expectations is more complex. Holding high expectations of children generally has a powerful effect on their learning (D.E.S., 1989, pp. 31–4). If we accept that children need their 'important people's' acceptance and approval, it's not hard to see why this is. Children must meet those expectations – or at least be seen to try to do so – in order to retain the acceptance and approval that they need.

It is most important that our expectations of children grow out of our knowledge of their abilities, achievements and interests. Watching and listening to children must form the basis of our expectations of them; otherwise, there is a danger that children may become overwhelmed by inappropriately high expectations. When this happens, children may no longer feel able to explore, experiment and make 'safe' mistakes from which they can learn. They may cease to struggle for 'mastery' and become 'helpless'.

Some adults are so acutely aware of this pitfall, and of children's need for acceptance and approval, that their expectations are disastrously low. In addition, praise may be offered constantly and indiscriminately, rather than as a result of real effort and achievement. The likely result is that children are not challenged to develop real knowledge, understanding and skills; and, in addition, there is a danger that they will develop an inflated and unrealistic idea of their own ability and potential which becomes a major obstacle to their learning progress. Also, these children tend to be either insensitive to any sort of censure or extremely vulnerable to the slightest criticism. They do not have that inner core of self-confidence which enables them to accept criticism and use it positively.

Components of self-esteem

Some very general statements can usefully be made about self-esteem: what it is, what it does and how it develops. Firstly, high self-esteem – or positive self-concept – is reflected in the possession of a secure sense of identity, and an ability to acknowledge and value our own efforts and achievements. Secondly, high self-esteem provides confidence, energy and optimism. Thirdly, high self-esteem is promoted by positive self-experiences (Curry and Johnson, 1990). The way in which Lily, Dan and Imran tackled designing a den indicated high levels of self-esteem in those children. They knew what they wanted, and they went about the task with confidence, energy and optimism.

Self-esteem is a complex concept. The critical components ebb and flow at different stages of development, but none the less are life-long issues, with their roots in the early years. As already mentioned in Chapter 1, Curry and Johnson have described these components as control and power, competence, values and acceptance. It is interesting to compare these components of self-esteem with the components of progression towards free-flow play, i.e. exploring, skills and competences, and ultimately the combination of competence with feelings and ideas. It would seem that there is much common ground between the development of free-flow play and the acquisition of high self-esteem. All four components of self-esteem are important; and, although one or other of three aspects – control and power, competence and value – may be dominant at different stages of a child's development, the fourth component – acceptance – appears to be crucial throughout.

Competition

Observations of babies, toddlers and young children reveal that they are predominantly concerned with gaining control, over themselves, over objects and over other people. Tiny babies struggle to control the movements of their hands and to lift up their heads; later, they spend hours on end investigating what happens when they drop, push or reach for. They engage in power-battles with parents, brothers and sisters, and their sense of self develops partly as a result of their success or failure with these things.

Later still, children begin to measure themselves, both in relation to their own knowledge and expectations of themselves, and in relation to each other. Some children become increasingly competitive, frequently comparing themselves with others; this is the way that they have learned to achieve their sense of worth or non-worth. Other children depend more on their inner sense of power and control. These children have been helped to learn about directing their own behaviour, managing the things they want to do and learning new knowledge and skills in collaboration with others. Lily, Dan and Imran's approach to den-making reflected this second approach.

There are disadvantages in encouraging children to compare themselves with others. Firstly, having winners necessitates having losers, and children who see themselves as losers do not generally learn happily, confidently or competently. Secondly, even the winners lose out. Such an approach only encourages them to be better than others; it does not expect or encourage a child's personal best, and this is to aim for lower than the summit.

It is often argued that competition is necessary, and so it is. But the most effective competition in the long term, and the sort that is most effective for all children, is the 'winners all' kind. This is when children are consistently engaged in winning against their own previous best.

Genuine praise

Self-esteem is related to our sense of significance and value. However, ideas about helping children to experience themselves as valuable and competent individuals have been open to misconception and trivialisation. For instance, the use of strategies such as habitual empty praise, gold stars, smiley stickers and meaningless statements, are more likely to feed children's self-preoccupation and narcissism than to help them form a genuine sense of their own worth (Docking, 1980).

Our responses to children have to be founded on realities if they are to carry meaning and avoid confusion and damage. This is one of the reasons why the recognition and acceptance of children's schemas can be such a useful and powerful way of looking at children. Strong self-esteem in children comes from living with people who understand, accept and support them on the basis of reality.

10

Adults aiming high

– AT THE BOTTOM OF THE DEEP BLUE SEA –

❝ It was cold and wet all this week, and the day I went to nursery with Lily was the coldest and wettest. All the children stayed in, and lots of them were playing on the big hollow wooden blocks, making a boat.

Lily played with them for a while, but the children weren't really playing with each other. One boy was being really bossy and he was telling everyone what to do; he was doing all the best things himself, like being the driver. Lily soon got fed up and went off to do some painting. Some of the others stayed there a long time, though. The teacher helped them make a flag for the boat, and they had the steering wheel, and they got some paper plates and things out of the junk modelling box and had a pretend picnic.

There's always a group-time every day, when the children talk about things with the teacher and have songs and stories. Most of the children at Lily's group-time had been pretending in the boat, but the bossy boy wasn't there. One of the girls had made a little puppet on a lolly stick, and it had yellow wool for its hair. When she saw the puppet, Lily's teacher said it reminded her of something, and when they'd finished their milk and sung the song about the bottom of the deep, blue sea and it was story-time, she said it was like something that has long fair hair and a fish's tail instead of legs! The children all knew she meant a mermaid, and then she said she was going to tell them a story about a family of sailors, and there was a mermaid in the story, too.

The teacher must have made up the story as she went along, because it was bit like when the children were pretending. Right at the beginning, as soon as she said something about the sailors having a picnic, Dan said, 'You're thinking about our one!' and he was really pleased.

When they came to the picnic bit of the story, the teacher asked them what they thought sailors like to eat. Lily said, 'Fish', quite loudly but Dan said, 'Worms', even louder. The teacher laughed at Dan's worms and she made the sailors in the story take their spades and tramp off to the fields to dig up worms for their picnic and put them in a little pot. That made Dan really pleased with his idea, and the children thought it was funny. Then the teacher made a pretend fishing rod by tying a piece of string to the end of a stick, and she made the sailor in the story catch the mermaid by mistake.

When the sailors were wondering whether she'd be good to eat, I thought Lily's and Amy's eyes would fall out of their heads, they were listening so hard. But the teacher made one of the sailors notice that she was frightened and be friends with her, so they decided to catch some proper fish instead, and she was safe.

In the story all sorts of things happened; the teacher showed them how to make lots of paper fishes at once, by folding the paper before you cut the fish shape, and the sailors had an argument about how many fishes they had caught, so they had to count them lots of times. The teacher made a pretend bonfire with some little sticks from the bush outside, and in the story they swam to a desert island and made a special shelter for sleeping. Then they took it in turns to look after each other by keeping a lookout for wild animals, and then they had to agree about what to have for breakfast. In the story, one of the sailors wanted to go home to his mum, and all the others made sure he was all right until the aeroplane came to rescue them.

Some days, the teacher makes up stories, and some days she just tells them or reads them from books. After the sailor story nearly all of the children wanted to go straight back to the blocks, and it was really interesting. Their pretending was different – much more with each other than before, pretending and making things that had been in the story and making up new things as well, like a monster that came out of the sea.

After a little while, the bossy boy came back again, and I thought he might spoil it. Amy was doing the steering, and the boy tried to push her out of the way. I was just going to stop him, when she looked him right in the eye and said, 'It's my turn'. The boy looked at her and looked at the wheel and the other children watching, and he didn't say anything, he just went off and joined the picnic! I saw the teacher give him a big smile, so she must have been pleased with him for doing that. **?**

Children are encouraged to learn when someone knows what they especially want to do and can nearly manage, and helps them to manage it successfully

Ways of helping children's learning

How children learn and *what* they learn go hand in hand. Two strategies can help to achieve this balance of how and what. First, we can look for ways in which we can identify, support and extend those things that children *want* to do, and having an understanding of schemas helps with this (Athey, 1990). Second, we can look for ways to identify, support and extend those things that children can *nearly* do (Vygotsky, 1978). Here, adults can help by having an understanding of the development of children's self-esteem, with its components of acceptance, power and control, competence and values (Curry and Johnson, 1990).

Children feel empowered to struggle with what they can nearly do when they know they are accepted, when they feel a sense of power and control, when they have sufficient competence, and when their efforts are valued. Our role as supporting adults can include watching and listening, questioning, accepting and encouraging, giving help when it is genuinely needed, enabling and encouraging reflection and planning, and recognising, valuing and applauding only *real* efforts and achievements.

The teacher's watching and listening was helpful because of the ideas she was able to give the children as a result. She had observed their interests and the level at which they would be likely to operate. Her interest and encouragement during the group-time helped them to talk to each other and to her about what had happened and what they wanted to do. Once they had the ideas, the addition of a blanket here and a few sticks there was enough for them to get on. The children needed something to pretend with, but nothing complicated.

Using puppets, either home-made or bought, can be a good way of introducing issues and ideas in a neutral way. If the puppet has been made by a child, as the mermaid puppet was, using it in this way can be particularly effective for children.

Lily's teacher had watched the children pretending and had noticed what they wanted to do and some of the problems they were having. Their needs had included a few props and some ways of dealing with situations. She fulfilled these needs, and once she had given them some ideas and suggestions, the children could continue to elaborate for themselves. They used her support, and took her ideas further.

The teacher's watching and listening served another purpose. Without being inhibited by it, the children were conscious of her attention and were supported by that. Sometimes this 'containing' function can be provided by a more able child. Vygotsky (1978, p. 87) describes children solving problems with adults' – or more able peers' – assistance. This is not the sort of helping where we do the difficult things *for* children, sometimes suggesting that, if they watch, one day they will be able to do it. The essence of this other sort of help is that the learners are the 'doers', while the supporters watch, *with appropriate optimism*. This appropriate optimism is the key to the process; it is the supporter's (realistic) confidence in the learner's ability that can affect the learner's self-expectation and enable the learner to break new ground.

– *FRIDAY NIGHTS AT HOME* –

❝ *Everybody's always in on Friday nights – the first part of Friday nights, anyway. The kids' dad really minds about it. He says it's important that everybody can talk about things and that we all listen to each other. That's why we all have our meal together on Fridays; Mum says it's the only time she knows we're all going to see each other, and sometimes she cooks special things, if she hasn't been too busy.*

I wouldn't miss it, anyway. There's Mum, the kids' dad, Lily, Joe and me. Sometimes there's a grown-up friend of Mum's or their dad's as well, but Mum and their dad don't talk to their friends instead of us; everybody joins in together. I like listening to everybody talking and I like watching Joe, too. Last Friday, he had his drink out of a glass for the first time, just like the rest of us; everybody cheered, and he was really proud of himself.

We had a big discussion that evening about when Lily pretended sailors at the nursery – Lily said it was her favourite, and told them all about it. I said, 'What about when you played moving house with Henna?' And Lily laid that was her favourite, too. Then Mum said weren't they both about the same thing, really about taking things from one place to another? Lily said, 'I like doing it,' and Mum said, 'I know,' and smiled at her. Then Lily said, 'Henna likes boxes – and the shopping basket.' And Mum said, 'We'll have to give her the bag to carry when she comes to the seaside with us next week.'

Then we all talked about what going to the seaside would be like, and what we wanted to do. Lily said she wanted to take her dolls in their buggy, and Mum said couldn't we take them without the buggy and Lily said, 'No!' very loudly. Her dad said he hoped they'd still have the coconut shy on the pier and the rifle range. Mum said she couldn't understand why he liked those things, and she was going to look for that wonderful machine that makes fresh doughnuts with lots of jam in the middle. They asked me next, and I said I like those train things that go up and down, and Lily said, 'That's at the fair,' and Joe jigged up and down and said, 'Train, train.' Then Mum grinned at him and said, 'We'll just take the Duplo, that'll keep you happy'. Joe looked anxious, so she said, 'Ice-cream?' and he jigged again.

Then the kids' dad said that he'd heard Lily's teacher talking about the way some children specially like doing the same sort of thing a lot of the time and that it's about patterns and the way children think about things. 'You and Lily's Henna think about things inside other things,' he said to Mum, 'and I like throwing and shooting and kicking footballs, all about moving lines.' They started arguing about whether he liked those things specially because he's a dad, but then they both laughed.

After that, it was time for pudding, and they laughed again because Mum had made her favourite, which is apple pasties with sultanas inside. Dad said he'd just remembered Lily's teacher saying that some children like taking things from one place to another and that must be the pattern that Lily has. Then I thought that when it's Lily's birthday next week, I'll give her the little rucksack I saw in the luggage-shop window, and then she can collect stones and things on the beach and bring them back safely. If Henna comes with us, perhaps I'd better get one for her too; she'd love putting things in it, and then they can carry their own treasures, all the way home.

'Talk about my day,' Lily said in bed that night. She always says that at bed-time, and you have to start with when she got up and go through everything that's happened. Sometimes you can skip bits, or she interrupts with things you didn't know. She really likes the naughty bits – and the times when people have been pleased with her. She likes talking about when she was upset, too, like the time Dan wasn't her friend any more because she'd had the best bike. Talking about it seems to make her feel better. Last Friday, she told me all about her new friend at school, Nicholas, who has a special wheelchair and looks funny. Lily says the other children don't play with him *much, but the other day he let her put all her things on his lap so she could take them outside, and now he's her friend. And last Friday she wasn't going to go to sleep until she'd told me all over again about what she and Henna are going to do at the seaside!*　❯

Recognising and supporting the development of children's patterns of learning, or schemas, leads to high self-esteem

Using schemas

Everybody needs the feeling that they are accepted, understood and valued. The recognition and acceptance by adults of children's schematic patterns contributes to these feelings in children. Schemas are at the heart of children's individuality, and so to recognise and support them appropriately is to recognise and support the child on a very fundamental level.

Using our knowledge of schemas can also make it much easier to help children develop skills and competence. Dan's hand-eye co-ordination will improve if we give him the new set of skittles, because his particular schema is a 'trajectory' one. Jessica's hand-eye co-ordination needs improvement too, but she is unlikely to show much interest in skittles. The way to encourage her to concentrate on hand-eye co-ordination for long enough to show a significant improvement, is to introduce her to the new construction set, possibly asking her to check that all the pieces fit together. She is likely to tackle this with concentration and persistence, because her schema is concerned with connecting.

Children planning and reflecting

Thinking and talking about what is *going* to happen is an important stage in the cycle of learning. There is now a growing emphasis among teachers on ways in which children can be more closely involved in the planning of their work; and everyone who makes a practice of this involvement will be in no doubt about its value (Lally, 1991, p. 69). Lily's appreciation of her day at the seaside, and her use of time on that day, will have been sharpened by the family discussion at tea the Friday before. This sort of approach, helping children to 'look ahead', is instrumental in nurturing a 'mastery' approach to learning, rather than a 'helpless' approach.

Less recognised, as yet, is the value of reflection with children. On a very ordinary level, it can be seen that occasions for talking over children's successful experiences with them are likely to raise their confidence, optimism and self-esteem. In addition, to be supported and encouraged in thinking and talking about unsuccessful or painful experiences means that children are much more likely to be able to learn from them positively.

The pressures of modern living and teaching make it increasingly difficult to pause to reflect with children. There seems always to be too much to do and too little time. In schools, it is common to see lessons which end with clearing up after the practical work is finished, and the time for important discussion about the children's experiences is missed (Driver, 1983). Activity by itself is not enough; it is the sense that is made of activity that matters.

Bed-time is often a good time for looking back over things. The next day is probably too late, and it's often hard to think about how and why something happened while still angry, hurt or elated. Bed-time offers enough detachment, but not too much; it also offers security. Children tend to feel comparatively secure at bed-time, possibly because the time, the place and the people are usually the same. Honest reflection does require an element of security. We all need to feel safe to think about mistakes, to feel proud of successes and to make useful connections between what has happened and what we will do next.

It is harder for staff to establish such a sense of security in a school setting, but the same principles can be made to apply – same times, same places, same people. This can represent quite a challenge in terms of organisation and management, but it is one worth tackling. We need to look for ways of establishing opportunities for reflection and planning. Does our organisation lend itself to this sort of provision? Do we already have situations which could, with a little adjustment, be used in this way? What about, for instance, an approach to school meals which encourages and enables conversation and discussion?

Regular opportunities to review and discuss past experiences, and to look forward together with others to new ones, are of great value. They can make a world of difference to such factors as children's aspirations, motivation, socialisation and self-esteem. It is these factors that are claimed to be the most important learning in pre-school education (Ball, 1994, p. 22).

Eating together

We recognise that 'doing' is an important part of the learning process. Time for play, when children are 'doing' at their highest level, is quality time for children. But time spent in looking backwards and forwards is quality time too. This is no less true at home than at school, where all too often the pace and pressure of life means that we see very little of our families in situations where we can make the most of being together. How can families make sure, for the sake both of adults and of children, that they have regular 'quality time' together?

One answer – Lily's dad's answer – is regular family meals. For some families, this means every day, and they are fortunate if the pattern of all their lives makes this practical. For others, it is harder; maybe working hours are variable, or perhaps someone – the baby or the adult on a night shift – is always asleep. These sorts of problems may result in less frequent family meals. There is no doubt that, for many families, eating together regularly presents real problems; but it's worth trying to get around the problems at least sometimes, so that families have a time when everyone can talk about their day (like Lily), and maybe share their feelings, hopes and plans.

Many adults – and indeed many older children – say that their experiences of eating together have not produced these benefits; that on the contrary, family meals tend to result in misunderstandings, stress and indigestion. Perhaps, for them, meals have not been thought of as times for listening, affirming, supporting and discussing, as well as eating. There are factors, too, that get in the way of family meals. Often it isn't that families have decided not to eat together, but that other things just seem to happen. Maybe it's someone's favourite television programme, or perhaps the children are in bed. Alternatively, perhaps the children are not in bed, but we wish they were, so we feed them quickly and get firm about bed-time. Sometimes houses don't seem to be designed with family meals in mind; there isn't enough space for everyone to sit down together, or the only big table is needed for other things. Maybe there needs to be some discussion, among the older people in the family at least, about the possibilities and pleasures of eating together.

– FUN AND FIREWORKS –

❝ It's nearly the summer holidays, and last week was the nursery picnic. It's a good thing there's quite a bit of space outside at that nursery because lots of families were there, and all the teachers and their families, and even some 'old' families from other years. It was a really warm evening, and there were loads of children and babies – all the nursery ones, and brothers and sisters, too.

I helped to get things ready, but there wasn't much to do after the nursery was tidied up at the end of the afternoon. We took all the tables outside and put them end to end with pretty paper on them; and we blew up lots of balloons and hung them on the posts and pillars and on the branches of the tree. Henna and Imran's mums had been cooking with the children in the afternoon, making samosas, and we put those on plates and got the orange squash ready. Jessica's dad brought two round lemon tarts that he'd made for the picnic, and Lily and me cut them up into equal pieces. After that, people started to come, and they all brought things for everybody to eat. We put the food out on the long table on nursery plates, so everybody could help themselves.

Mum and Joe arrived; Mum had brought the salad that we'd made last night and a blanket for us to sit on. Lily gave Joe a big hug and took him off to play with her friends in their camp. That was the last we saw of them for ages, and when their dad came later, nearly all the food was gone, but Mum had saved him some. He brought his friends Andy and Steve; Andy had what Mum calls his squeeze-box with him, for playing dancing music, and Steve had his fiddle. When Lily saw it, she rushed off to get her *friends, and when he started playing, they held hands and jumped about pretending to dance; and people stood around in a circle and clapped.*

After a while, Lily's teacher asked Andy if we could do a proper dance, and Andy said he and Steve could play one if someone would stand in the middle and teach people what to do. Mum's friend Wendy said she knew some dances and that she'd help. We had to have partners; some people joined in, and some just wanted to watch. I was going to watch, but the kids' dad said I was his partner and Mum was with Dan's mum, and everybody got in a muddle and laughed a lot. Soon, Wendy said she knew we could do it properly, and then we did, and it was really fun. After that, we got lots of children to come and dance as well, and that was the best part. We just did the easy bits and the going round and round bits, and the children loved it. I had Joe, and Mum had Lily. Joe could only go round and round with me hanging on to him tight, but he really loved the music and the jigging about.

When Andy was putting his squeeze-box away he said if we liked, he could give us a tape of the music. Then when the children had got really good at going up and down and round and round, we could decide what order we wanted to do it in and make up our own nursery dance. Lily's teacher thought that was a great idea; she said it would be really good to know how to do some dances properly. And it would be even more fun, once we knew how to do them well enough, to play around with the dances and make our own.

It was nearly dark by the time everyone had finished eating and dancing and chatting and playing, and some of the babies were asleep. Lily and Joe were wide awake, though. We were just thinking about going home, when everyone had a lovely surprise. One of the teachers (not Lily's) was leaving the nursery because her family was moving, and she had brought some fireworks for a special treat, to say goodbye to everyone. There were Roman Candles and Silver Rain and Catherine Wheels; and this teacher had made sure that the fireworks had no really loud bangs, so nobody was frightened. The last one was a really amazing rocket; it whooshed up with a sort of swishing noise and covered the sky with tiny little gold and silver stars that floated away gently in the dark. **?**

Children learn well with a combination of appropriately high expectations and appropriately high self-esteem

Self-esteem in early childhood education and care settings

In schools and early years settings, there are a number of practical strategies that are relevant to the ways in which children learn to see themselves. It can be illuminating to ask ourselves some questions, for instance about organisation, adults' approaches, and assessment and recording arrangements. Are there times for all the children to listen and be heard, about how they feel and what they have done? Do all the children have opportunities to make genuine choices? How much are all children trusted and given responsibility?

In relation to adults, are staff aware of their priorities? Do they give clear messages about those priorities to children and parents? Do children have an 'important person'? What is that person's role and responsibility? What behaviour management strategies are there? What support is there for children as they move to their next school? Are these strategies and arrangements consistent with developing positive self-concept in children?

Assessment and recording arrangements carry a world of hidden messages for children and parents. Is a positive model used, one which identifies children's special strengths as well as areas for support? Is there accurate and detailed information about children? Do adults make sure that children share their successes, both with their parents and with each other?

These questions raise some of the issues which have a direct bearing on how children learn to see themselves, and which make a major impact on children's learning dispositions. More about dispositions is to be found in Part 6. Attention to these sorts of details may have a profound effect on children's approach to learning. Our attention to them is surely the entitlement of every child.

Working together

From birth onwards, an increasing variety of people will be involved with each child. As well as the usual widening circle of family and friends, there will be those involved in the child's health, welfare and education. Parents are generally the most, and sometimes the only, permanent players in this shifting cast of adults. Increasingly, this is being recognised and used positively by those who work with young children, for instance in the use of parent-held child health and development records.

Continuity and co-ordination between all the people who work with children is crucially important (David, 1990, p. 153). Unless we have an awareness of the unseen pieces in the jigsaw of a child's life, we may not be especially effective, helpful or reassuring to that child. This is particularly important for children who are meeting adults from different cultures than their own and for children with special needs. All children need continuity and co-ordination; but the more adults there are involved with a child, and the more diverse they are, the more urgent this becomes. These are issues that the Sure Start programmes have been set up to address. At all levels, we need to be working towards a more coherent experience for young children and their families.

Freedom and responsibility

Much of this book is about achieving a balance in situations that affect us all. It is about how feelings affect learning, and how learning affects feelings; about meeting

individual needs within the wider context of the family and society, and about considering the needs of others without losing sight of the individual; about the way in
which our responses to children affect their development, and how their development dictates our responses to them

It has been argued that satisfying learning experiences in early childhood result
in children who want to learn and who see the point in struggling to do so. Teachers of older children, as well as parents and employers, will certainly testify to the
extreme importance of developing these positive learning dispositions, in which
children understand the value of learning in terms of usefulness and pleasure.

There has been considerable emphasis on children's need for understanding and
for freedom to 'be themselves'. However, Chapters 5 and 6 also stress the importance of children's perceptions of themselves, not only as individuals, but also as
part of a larger group – of the family, the community, our multi-cultural society,
ultimately of all humanity. At the heart of this balance between the needs of the
individual and society lie the issues of responsibility and freedom. To be given total
responsibility and no freedom seriously inhibits children's ability to develop and to
learn, and would rarely now be advocated. Complete freedom, together with few or
no expectations of responsibility, is a more frequent state of affairs, but unfortunately the price tends to be unhappy anarchic children now, and disaffected, anti-
social adults to come.

Children do need freedom. But not total freedom, which lacks the security of containment, the reassurance of limits, the way towards self-control. Our greatest challenge is to try to achieve for children an appropriate combination of freedom and
responsibility. This is how to make the most of early learning – and how to be ready,
willing and able for school, and ready, willing and able for life.

POSTSCRIPT TO PART 5: REAL SELF ESTEEM

Living or working with young children?
Questions to think about . . .

> **Children are encouraged to learn when someone knows what they especially want to do and can nearly manage, and helps them to manage it successfully**

1. What theories and strategies can we use in order to discover what children especially want to do, and can nearly manage?

> **Recognising and supporting the development of children's patterns of learning, or schemas, leads to high self-esteem**

2. How can we recognise and support the development of children's schemas?

> **Children learn well with a combination of appropriately high expectations and appropriately high self-esteem**

3. What can be done by 'important adults' to support the development of appropriately high self-esteem in young children?

RECOMMENDED FURTHER READING

For sharing with children . . .

Briggs, R. (1978), *The Snowman*, London, Hamish Hamilton
Another classic, the enchanted friendship between the snowman and the boy gives us a story of boredom and excitement, fun and fear, suspense and delight, love and loss. And all without a word of text, which makes this a wonderful book for chatting about and elaborating on the story, and picking up on the experiences and preoccupations of the listening child.

For a good read . . .

Dowling, M. (2000), *Young Children's Personal, Social and Emotional Development*, London, Paul Chapman Publishing
Marion Dowling's book opens with a strong chapter, 'Confident Children', which elaborates on many of the issues raised in this section. This very helpful and accessible book shows how children can be helped to develop confidence, social skills and independence.

For reference . . .

Early Childhood Education Forum (1998), *Quality in Diversity in early learning*, London, National Children's Bureau
This framework for early childhood practitioners was developed by a consortium of major UK organisations concerned with the care and education of young children. Representing a new coherence in the thinking of early years practitioners and with a structure of foundations, goals and entitlements reminiscent of Te Whariki, it offers a way of understanding more clearly and valuing more explicitly the richness and complexity of young children's learning.

PART 6

READY, WILLING AND ABLE

11

Children ready for school, ready for life

– LISA COMES TO STAY –

❛ The day after the picnic at Lily's nursery, Lisa came to stay. Mum says she's a sort of cousin, something to do with Mum's family. Lisa's two years older than me and goes to College, and she's come to see Lily and Joe. She says she has to watch them for her college work, and she wants to come with us when we do things. Mum says I should talk to Lisa about Lily and Joe because I know so much about them now – not so much as her though, but when I said that she said she was too busy to talk to Lisa. I'm pleased she thinks I can do it instead of her. Anyway, Lisa's cool.

Last night we were having bed-time stories, and it was Joe's turn to choose. When he picked out the same old 'Where's the Bear?' story again we all groaned, but he really wanted it, and then he had to have it three times! It was Lily's turn to tell it and she kept skipping a page, and every time Joe screamed at her. She was teasing him, making him scream on purpose, especially when she started leaving out the song. I had to promise we'd play the game about it tomorrow, to calm him down.

Lisa was really surprised that he still wanted that story when he knew it by heart already – and that he really minds about books when he's so small. But Lily told her that Joe's always had books and stories, since the day he was born. ❜

> **Talking, listening, playing and singing together, and sharing books every day . . . from birth all children need opportunities to do these things, with people they love and admire who recognise, value and encourage their efforts and achievements**

What do we know about babies' brains?

The last ten years have produced more knowledge about the brain and how it develops than scientists had gleaned in the previous several centuries (Shore 1997).

However, there has been a debate, fuelled by the media, as to the significance of these findings for the ways in which we educate and care for the youngest children. On the one hand are writers and speakers who claim that new brain research demonstrates the importance of the first three years for brain development and that certain experiences make a difference. On the other hand are scientists who urge caution, saying that we do not yet know enough about brain development to assert in any reliable way that certain experiences are necessary.

Dr. Anne Meade's conclusions for our practice (2000) form part of Chapter 12. The focus in this chapter is on babies and young children themselves, beginning with a vivid analogy of the brain at birth given by Guy Claxton (1997, p. 137) in his book 'Hare Brain, Tortoise Mind':

> *When a human baby is born, there are certain genetically determined frameworks that serve to impose a general structure on the brain, but much remains unfixed. The brain is like a vast lecture theatre of students on their first day at university: full of potential friendship, but as yet strangers to each other. After a few weeks however, each student has begun to belong to a number of different evolving circles of acquaintances: study groups, sports teams, neighbourhoods and clubs. Just so, every neuron in the brain comes to belong to a variety of developing clusters, each of which is bound together in such a way that stimulation of one member, or a small group of members, is likely to lead to 'recruitment' of the others. And the major reason why they tend to become associated is simply that they are active at the same time. Communication becomes more selective, and information begins to flow, throughout the neural community as a whole, along more stable channels.*

In 'Re-thinking the Brain', Rima Shore (1997, pp. ix–xi) summarises five things that we now know about the development of young children's brains, as follows:

1. Human development hinges on the interplay between nature and nurture.
2. Early care has a decisive and long-lasting impact on how people develop, their ability to learn, and their capacity to regulate their own emotions.
3. The human brain has a remarkable capacity to change, but timing is crucial.
4. There are times when negative experiences or the absence of appropriate stimulation are more likely to have sustained and serious effects.
5. Evidence amassed over the last decade points to the wisdom and efficacy of prevention and early intervention.

The UK House of Commons Education and Employment Select Committee received a briefing for their enquiry from Sarah-Jayne Blakemore (2000), who gave three well-established findings in developmental neurobiology, as follows:

- First, starting in infancy and continuing into later childhood, there is a dramatic increase in the number of connections (synapses) between brain cells (neurons). This 'synaptic proliferation' is followed by a period of synaptic elimination, or 'pruning', in which frequently used connections are strengthened and infrequently used connections are eliminated.

- Second, there are 'critical periods' when the development of sensory and motor systems in the brain depends on experience.
- Third, in rats at least, complex, or enriched, environments cause new synapses to form.

She continues:

However, many neuro-scientists believe that not enough is presently known about brain development to link that understanding directly to instruction and educational practice.

But the evidence does seem to generate a consensus about one thing, which Anne Meade (2000) puts very simply: 'Experience shapes how our genes are expressed'. This brings us back to the question of experience.

The source of the most significant experiences for children under three is other people. Both parents and practitioners watch children in order to try to understand how they think, and how their thinking can be supported and extended. Perhaps we should not be expecting brain research to tell us what to do with the youngest children, but rather we could ask: 'What can brain research contribute to our understanding about what is going on inside children's heads as we watch them?' Then it is up to us – the people who live and work with babies and young children – to ask *ourselves* what the answers mean, and what we should do about it.

What do we need to know about learning?

So our questions about the implications of nature and nurture and the interaction between the child's inner and outer world are ones that we should be asking of ourselves as educators, rather than of scientists. But we need all the evidence that science can give us, to inform our deliberations on how best to help children to learn. We can use hypotheses from neuroscience to help us reflect on our own observations of children, and to help us to find answers to some of our own more pressing questions. Here are a few questions which new knowledge might help us to answer, and of course there are many more:

- Are there best times for particular sorts of learning? Best environments? Best people to learn with?
- Are the best learning environments more likely to be achieved by *enrichment* (adding to children's normal experiences – but can one over-do it?) Or by *conservation* (preserving certain aspects of the young child's environment that are being eroded by our twenty-first century way of life; for instance, opportunities to 'play out', as it was called)?

- What is known about the apparently different learning styles of boys and girls? Does this have any significance in providing for children in the context of changing family patterns?
- How important is a properly integrated curriculum in the early years? Is it possible that the way young children think means that teaching 'subjects' in the Foundation Stage could be counter-productive?
- Should early education focus more on learning to ask the right questions than on learning the right answers?
- Babies and very young children are voracious learners. Why do children sooner or later seem to lose this powerful disposition to learn? What needs to happen for a child to be as enthusiastic about learning at twelve as he or she was at two?

Why involve parents?

Nearly all children spend almost all of their time from birth to school at home. This is especially the case from birth to three years. During this time, babies and young children learn an astonishing amount, about themselves, the people around them, and the world in which they live. From total helplessness and in an amazingly short time, they learn to walk, to talk, and to take part in family life in increasingly sophisticated ways.

In spite of what we know about the rapid rate of brain development and of these solid early achievements, government-funded support for children's development, and the literature about early learning, appears to reflect a view that 'education' begins sometime after the child's third birthday, when he or she makes contact with some sort of education provision outside the home. This does not of course make sense in terms of the real lives of children at home, from the day they are born. An enormous opportunity exists to lay solid foundations for later learning throughout life by acknowledging parents' crucial role from birth. Parents are the real specialists – in their own children. They are the people 'in the hot seat' when this crucial 'foundation' learning is taking place. 'Sure Start' and other programmes in the UK are beginning to acknowledge this and to develop ways of supporting parents, but there is a long way to go before even a modest level of support is offered universally.

Whether we like it or not, babies and young children do not wait to learn until we are ready to teach them. They get straight on with it from day one, learning from all the people, places and events around them from the very start. Nor are they selective, picking up only the things we would like them to absorb. They are like little sponges, soaking up everything indiscriminately. Joe may know a very wide range of stories and songs, but he also knows that if he makes a big fuss he'll probably get something he wants, like playing his favourite game. He's getting very good at telling Mum at bed-time all about his day and what happened, but he was listening to Dan telling Lily about the playground yesterday and his account is likely to be sprinkled with the swear-words that are now part of Dan's and Lily's vocabulary. (Dan and Lily have also learned something else, which is that grown-ups don't like to hear children using those words even though they themselves do sometimes – but Joe is too young for this subtlety.)

The only way to make sure that *all* babies and young children are given the support that will help them to do well at school is to make sure that *all* parents have access to the information and ideas they need to enable them to provide that support. Currently only a minority of parents access this information. There is a need for accessible materials that all parents can use easily, such as those developed by the Pen Green Centre (1997), the PEEP project (Roberts 2000), and the SHELLS project in Australia.

Materials like these are based on what the youngest children love doing with adults, building on many of the things that all parents normally do from day to day at home, regardless of where they live and their circumstances. Young children all love to have someone who listens, and they all love lots of talk, stories, songs and rhymes and playing together. These are the things that help children to make a flying start.

– VISITING DAN –

❛ *Dan's off to Big School after the summer – and just before the end of term he had to go and look at his classroom and see his teacher. Lily and Mum went with him to drop him off. Mum said that now Lily has seen where Dan will be, she can look forward to going there too, after Christmas. But Lily said she didn't want to go, and Mum said was it the big boys? Lily said yes; but I think she was jealous of Dan and feeling angry because he's going without her. Anyway Mum said not to worry, they'd be going to collect Dan lots of times next term so she'd soon get used to it. And Mum said she was going to help Dan's teacher sometimes and Lily could come too if she liked. Then Lily really cheered up, because she knew they'd let her play in the Home Corner in Dan's classroom, which is much more grown-up than the one at Nursery and has lots of books and things.*

Lisa said she thought Mum was really good, because at College they tell you that parents and teachers need to get to know each other and talk about the children's learning and progress, and that's what Mum's doing. She said that's what makes children feel safe to go to school, and then they can get on with learning. ❜

Wanting to learn makes all the difference to success

Learning dispositions . . . a goal of twenty-first century education?

Not only has there been an acknowledgement of the extraordinary competence of very young children, but also we have seen an important expansion in the view of the curriculum itself, in which children's personal, social and emotional development is seen as crucially important. However, children's *disposition* to learn has not been seen as a goal of education in itself. Here is how Lilian Katz (1993, p. 1) saw it:

> *One of the major questions to be addressed when developing a curriculum is, What should be learned? One way to answer this question (Katz, 1991) is to adopt at least four types of learning goals, those related to knowledge, skills, dispositions and feelings. The acquisition of both knowledge and skills is taken for granted as an educational goal, and most educators would also readily agree that many feelings (e.g. self-esteem) are also influenced by school experiences and are thus worthy of inclusion among learning goals. However, dispositions are seldom included, although they are often implied by the inclusion of attitudes (e.g. attitudes towards learning) as goals . . . it is possible to have skills and lack a taste for or habit of using them. Similarly, knowledge can be acquired without having the disposition to use it.'*

What difference would it make to the way schools operate if the first and most important question to be asked in formal assessments, linked to transitions (e.g. from home to nursery, from nursery to primary school, from primary to secondary school), was 'Does this child want to be here to learn?'

Lilian Katz (1993) points to the progress that has been made in relation to the goals for early education in recent decades. In addition to their physical development, we acknowledge the importance of children's social and emotional development, as well as what they know and can do. The contents of a range of current curriculum guidance publications and recently developed assessments confirm this to be the case, but as Katz points out there is one glaring omission. At no point in the assessment of children in the primary or secondary phases is there a requirement to ask the most fundamental question of all – does this child *want* to learn?

The question of children's learning dispositions is an important one that has been explored in a variety of ways, especially by Sylva (1994) and Katz (1995). In her book *Assessment in Early Childhood Settings* (2001, p. 23), Margaret Carr analyses the domains of learning dispositions as:

- taking an interest
- being involved
- persisting with difficulty or uncertainty
- communicating with others
- taking responsibility

Taking this analysis a step further, she proposes the categories of 'being ready', 'being willing', and 'being able', fitting the domains listed above into these stages of development. No-one engaged in supporting young children's learning could deny the extreme relevance of, say, being ready to take an interest, being willing to take an interest, and being able to do so; or of being ready, willing and able to communicate, and so on. This altogether new way of looking at outcomes of early childhood education and care is a thought-provoking alternative to the usual categories of language, mathematics etc. For anyone who might wonder whether this is merely to reach a starting point for early learning, here, for example, is how being ready, willing and able to persist with difficulty or uncertainty (an area closely related to self-esteem) is described:

- Readiness to persist, in which children are developing: enthusiasm for persisting with difficulty or uncertainty; assumptions about risk and the role of making a mistake in learning; a view of self as someone who persists with difficulty and uncertainty.
- Willingness to persist, in which children are developing: sensitivity to places and occasions in which it is worthwhile to tackle difficulty or uncertainty and to resist the routine.
- Ability to persist, in which children are developing: problem-solving and problem-finding knowledge and skills; experience of making mistakes as part of solving a problem.

This thinking highlights the complexity of learning dispositions, indicating some of the important elements contained within the simple question of whether or not a child wants to learn, and why. And that simple question is important in helping us to remain focused on some of the most effective things that help children to make a flying start.

Sure Start – developing ways of working together

It is very helpful for families with babies and young children needing support from a range of sources, if the various support services are able to co-ordinate and work together. Without such co-ordination, families already under pressure can feel harassed and discouraged by the number of service-providers with whom they are in contact. In such circumstances it is difficult for parents to feel any sense of ownership or control over both problems and solutions. One way of dealing with this in the UK has been the development of Sure Start programmes for 0s–3s, where the emphasis is on integrated support across the services; and, in Australia, initiatives such as Families First and Stronger Families and Communities Strategy. Sure Start programmes offer an exciting new way of supporting families with the youngest children, aiming to make a difference to children's physical development, their social and emotional development, how they learn and school readiness. Sure start programmes also aim to strengthen families and communities in a variety of ways including by working together with shared aims, objectives and targets.

This integrated approach to supporting families is underpinning the development of new collaborative strategies, with the intention of changing radically the provision that is offered to families. The Pen Green Centre has been blazing this trail for many years, working inspirationally to meet the needs of families and young children in an holistic way (Whalley, 1997). In this new way of working, health visitors, schools, family centres and voluntary bodies come together, providing a more 'seamless' service for children and families. Much will be learned from all this new work, and from the opportunities that are generated to identify those elements that are most effective in supporting families with the youngest children.

– THE TREASURE HUNT –

6 *Yesterday Lily wanted to meet her friends at the Adventure Playground – there's some holiday stuff going on there and they were going to do a Treasure Hunt. So we all went, and I looked after Joe while Lily did the Treasure Hunt with Lisa and Dan. Lisa said Lily was really fed up at first because they had to read and write things and it was difficult for Lily and at first she couldn't see the point. But then when she saw that the messages were how you did the Treasure Hunt, Lily stopped fussing and explained it all to the others in her team and got Lisa to help. In the end they won, and there was a photographer there who took their photographs for the paper. They all chose a prize out of the Treasure Hunt Box, and Lily chose a book about babies.*

When we got home Lily had to tell her dad all about it. When he said 'What was the Treasure then?' she showed him the book about babies that she had chosen, and he and Mum laughed at the idea of her thinking babies were treasures when she gets so cross with Joe. But she said now she's grown-up and knows about why you do reading and writing and things, she doesn't mind about Joe. She says she can explain grown-up things to him, like she did to the others today. I wonder what he'll think of that? 9

> **Self-confidence; the ability to listen and talk and get on with other people; interest in the world; understanding about the uses of reading, writing, numbers and books; the disposition to learn . . . this is how children make a flying start**

A new view of children?

Are children empty vessels that need to be filled up with knowledge, or do children possess astonishing knowledge, skills and understanding for their years – a concept of 'half full' rather than 'half empty'? Sensitive adults living with and caring for young children down the centuries have been surprised and delighted by their use of language, newly acquired skills and fresh view of the world. But it is only recently, as the imaging techniques of neuroscience begin to map the early development of the brain, that a more universal awareness of the competence and the potential of very young children is beginning to emerge.

Now we know that most of what children learn about the physical world is acquired by exploring, playing and observing the relations between objects. Even young babies learn about other people, naturally imitating their gestures, facial expressions and actions. They can tell the difference between facial expressions of happiness, sadness and anger, and their ability to understand other people's emotions continues to develop throughout the first few years of life. They begin to develop a 'theory of mind' at the age of about four, starting to realise not only that they believe certain things (e.g. I *think* Joe's book is in his room) but that people can have different beliefs from their own, and that they themselves can have different beliefs at different times (Blakemore, 2000). Children learn mainly through their own experiences of playing, exploring, everyday conversations and generally being with other people.

One of the most influential approaches to children's learning since the 1960s has been the provision for children under six years in Reggio Emilia in Northern Italy. The 'Reggio approach' has gained world-wide recognition for its inspirationally profound view of children as strong, powerful and competent learners, and its emphasis on community and citizenship. More is now known in the UK about this work as a result of the 'Hundred Languages of Children' exhibition. Loris Malaguzzi (1997, p. 117), founder of the Reggio approach to pre-school education, wrote:

> *Our image of children no longer considers them as isolated and egocentric, does not only see them as engaged in action with objects, does not emphasise only the cognitive aspects, does not belittle feelings or what is not logical and does not consider with ambiguity the role of the reflective domain. Instead our image of the child is rich in potential, strong, powerful, competent and most of all connected to adults and children.*

Early childhood has been described by Margaret Donaldson et al (1983) as

> *. . . a period of momentous significance for all people growing up in our culture . . . By the time this period is over, children will have formed conceptions of themselves as social beings, as thinkers, and as language users, and they will have reached certain important decisions about their own abilities and their own worth.*

The personal, social and emotional curriculum

These and many other positive views of children and how they learn – and indeed the broader perception of what they learn – have had a profound effect on views of teaching and learning. This change is clearly reflected in the most significant recent early childhood education curriculum documents. Possibly the most fundamental change has been the prominence now given to personal, social and emotional aspects of teaching and learning. With this new prominence comes a greater awareness both of outcomes in early childhood education and of the need to focus on the *processes* of learning in order to reach those outcomes.

An enormous upsurge of thinking, discussion and writing in relation to early learning is indicated by a wide range of new early years curriculum documents. These relate mainly to learning from three years, building on a long tradition of good practice in early childhood education while at the same time incorporating new evidence about child development, and new perspectives on goals for education in the twenty-first century. Inevitably there will be tensions and debates relating to the needs of young children, the most appropriate ways in which they can be met, and the right timing for meeting them. Also there is still comparatively little to support children's learning from birth to three, and for good reason. Here there is the added complexity that most of these children spend most of their time in the home with their parents. Their learning is inextricably woven into the fabric of the everyday life in the many rich and diverse parenting traditions of our multi-cultural society. Developing relevant and appropriate support for parents and carers in such very diverse cultures and circumstances will be both a vitally important and an enormously sensitive task.

However, there are now at least three important and profoundly influential curriculum documents, one from New Zealand and two from the UK. Each of these documents focuses in different ways on the processes of learning and on principles and goals. Principles, strands and goals rather than curriculum 'content' are the main focus of Te Whariki, the basis of the New Zealand early years curriculum which aims to enhance children's sense of themselves as capable people and competent learners. It is founded on the following aspirations for children:

> *To grow up as competent and confident learners and communicators, healthy in mind, body and spirit, secure in their sense of belonging and in the knowledge that they make a valued contribution to society.* (New Zealand Ministry of Education 1996, p. 9)

Te Whariki is built around the principles of empowerment, holistic development, family and community, and relationships. The strands within each of these principles are well-being, belonging, contribution, communication and exploration. Within each strand is a range of goals. It was developed specifically to be appropriate in all early childhood education settings in New Zealand, both Maori and non-

Maori. Focusing on structure and processes rather than content, this document offers insights in relation to identifying relevant and appropriate common ground for all children in a multi-cultural society.

Quality in Diversity (1998) is a framework for early childhood practitioners working with children from birth to eight. It was developed in England by the Early Childhood Education Forum, because of changes in family patterns and family roles, and to acknowledge the increasing richness and cultural diversity of British society, and the increasing number of children experiencing education and care in a wide range of settings. Other significant factors were recent legislation, training and assessment issues.

This framework has much in common with Te Whariki, incorporating three main elements: firstly, foundations for early learning – belonging and connecting, being and becoming, contributing and participating, being active and expressing, and thinking, imagining and understanding; secondly, goals for early learning; and thirdly, children's entitlements.

These two documents ultimately had a significant effect on the development of Curriculum Guidance for the Foundation Stage (2000). The subject of vigorous debate over a period of years, this document derives from Early Learning Goals (1999), and now constitutes the basis of the Foundation Stage curriculum for all children in England and Wales from three to six years. Although structured around much more 'subject-orientated' areas of learning, its aims, principles, and emphasis on parents as children's first and most enduring educators, resonate with the approaches of its predecessors and have been warmly welcomed by practitioners as a basis for good practice.

In particular, first and foremost of the areas of learning are personal, social and emotional development, which are described as:

> critical for very young children in all aspects of their lives and gives them the best opportunity for success in all other areas of learning. It is crucial that settings provide the experiences and support to enable children to develop a positive sense of themselves. (QCA 2000, p. 28)

Importance is given to a range of aspects of personal, social and emotional development. Within this area of the curriculum are included constructive relationships between adults and children, positive encouragement, time and space for children's own interests, developing autonomy and the disposition to learn, sensitively inclusive provision, and developing independence. Here in this government guidance, and echoing years of early education debate around the world, is a real recognition of the interdependence between the child's positive sense of self and the ability to learn successfully.

Howard Gardner, in 1993, wrote of 'throwing out limiting old assumptions and respecting the flexibility, creativity, adventurousness, resourcefulness and generativity of the young mind.' Now at the start of the twenty-first century, our understanding of children and their learning stands as never before in a place of tantalising opportunity. From Plato to the present day early childhood education, arguably the most important of human preoccupations, has never before been perceived as so vital. Never before has it been thought so promising a field of study, so appropriate a subject for investment and research, so important an area of employment, so fundamental for the present and for the future of our society. And never before has the challenge to early childhood educators been so great.

12

Adults ready, willing and able to help

– MUM DOES IT RIGHT! –

❝ We looked after Dan this week so his Mum could take their new baby to a group. Dan's mum's shy, and so Mum said she'd go too, just to help her get started. They came back with a tape of baby songs and a special song book to go with it, and they said the baby loved it. Lily had to put it on straight away. She says she needs one too! Mum said she'd better go to a group then, they do them for Lily's age as well and I could take her as I look after her such a lot.

They said there were lots of other mums and babies there who live round about, so Dan's mum can get to know some other people. A lady had come to see Dan's mum to tell her about it in case she wanted to go . . . she said it was all about helping your baby to learn, and that babies need lots of talking and singing and games, and books every day. She said talking to babies is what everybody does anyway, and going to the group makes people feel better about being a mum and everyone's welcome. That was when Dan's mum decided to give it a try.

They had a really good folder with ideas and stuff too . . . and when Mum looked at it with Dan's mum she laughed because there was a game in there about having a cardboard box with a hole in it and the baby puts things in and then takes the lid off and takes them out and does it all over again. She said it was Joe's favourite game for months and the cheapest toy he'd ever had. Then she looked at some more things in the folder and she was smiling. She said perhaps she'd done it right after all because she did lots of these things, and it was nice to see them all together in a book. And Lily got cross and said SHE did things right, not Mum . . . she's cross quite a lot these days, Mum says it's because she's left her nursery and not gone to school yet and she's feeling worried. Anyway Mum was nice to her and said yes, she'd be QUITE all right when she got to school with the others, because of all the games and books and things that she likes. Lily was happy then. ❞

Talking, listening, playing and singing together, and sharing books every day . . . from birth all children need opportunities to do these things, with people they love and admire who recognise, value and encourage their efforts and achievements

What do we know?

In her Fulbright Lecture (2000) entitled 'The Brain Debate', Dr Anne Meade concluded:

> There is a convergence of findings from neuroscience, cognitive science, development psychology and early childhood education research. Generally, there is agreement that enriched environments such as are found in high quality early childhood settings facilitate the adaptive changes to children's brains. The enrichment of social relationships – of adult-child interactions – is especially important, remembering of course that the brain is malleable and the changes in response to relationship experience can be both positive and negative for the child.

Meade suggests that brain research does validate and explain many observational/clinical findings, and that imaging research is showing where, when and what is unusual in brain functioning in people with learning and behavioural disorders. While emphasising that behavioural neuroscience is still in its infancy, she draws some tentative conclusions from research about appropriate early experiences for brain development which include the following:

- The quality of interpersonal relationships, i.e. adult-child interactions, is very important. An adult tuning into and responding to the child's mental state allows his or her brain to develop a capacity to balance emotions and thinking skills.
- Experiences for young children need to address their need for stimulation of all the senses and the associated brain regions. Multi-modal activity – involving the senses, motor skills and thinking – is important.
- Play addresses the brain's need for multi-sensory, multi-modal experiences. Animal studies suggest that the play needs to include social, complex and challenging experiences.
- Provision for the development of implicit memories is likely to be more fruitful than direct instruction, as the brain circuits for explicit memories do not mature until the age of 3 or 4 years. Implicit memories are built by diverse exposures to an array of inputs in naturalistic settings.

What can we do?

Knowing what will help each particular child to make a flying start at school and grow into a competent, confident adult is a complicated business, and depends to a large extent on the particular needs of the individual child and the expertise of parents and carers. The EPPE project (Sammons, et al, 1999) has shown that when children have had certain experiences in the earliest years at home, they will be in a better position to learn at school. Until recently it was thought that the strongest predictors of children's later achievements were the level of their parents' education, especially the mother's, and parents' occupational status. These are still known to be significant, but the list of experiences below were found to be more important even after parents' education and occupational status had been taken into account. The experiences are:

- Regular book-sharing
- Regular library visits
- Playing with letters or numbers
- Learning the alphabet
- Knowing various songs and rhymes

This list will not come as a surprise to people who are living and working with young children. 'Well we knew that already!' can be the response to findings that seem to confirm our common sense. It is important, however, that such findings can be put forward as the result of solid evidence rather than as a kind of folklore. Children's education and care should be based on a careful synthesis of the body of evidence we have, if we are to avoid placing them at the mercy of the winds of education 'fashion' and political change.

How can parents and carers help?

The parent or carer is the central person for the child in the external world as well as the internal one of the home. In the child's rapidly expanding world the parent or main carer is the continuity person, a child specialist in relation to *this* child. He or she also knows everyone who provides services – the health visitor, the child minder, the day-care superviser, the pre-school leader, the family centre staff, the teacher. This co-ordinating role is crucial, and many services work hard to acknowledge this and make the most of it. The Curriculum Guidance for the Foundation Stage (p. 9) has this to say about parents:

> *Parents are children's first and most enduring educators. When parents and practitioners work together in early years settings, the results have a positive impact on the child's development and learning. Therefore, each setting should seek to develop an effective partnership with parents. A successful partnership needs a two-way flow of information, knowledge and expertise.*

The Sure Start booklet entitled *Providing good quality childcare and early learning experiences through Sure Start* confirms:

> *A strong relationship with parents encourages continuity for the child, good communication, participation and ownership. In order to be involved, parents must have information.*
>
> (p. 24)

In its report on the Early Years, the House of Commons Education and Employment Select Committee (2000) has as opening section headings 'Parents' and 'Childminders'. This government report goes a step further in flagging up the crucial importance of very early learning at home. Peter Hannon (1995) proposed that all families do in fact provide children with the kinds of experiences that underpin literacy learning, and that the four key factors are providing children with opportunities, recognition of their achievements, everyday interactions, and modelling.

In the 'Learning Together' series (Roberts ed, 2000), the PEEP project has further developed this model as a basis for working with parents about supporting their children's self-esteem and learning dispositions, as well as their very early literacy and numeracy development. This is how the model is described in the introduction to each 'Learning Together' folder:

'Learning Together' covers the time from birth to school . . . It is based on four main ideas:

- Opportunities for learning and all-round development in everyday life
- Recognising and valuing children's efforts and achievements day by day
- Interactive everyday activities and experiences to do together
- Modelling or setting an example by adults can make all the difference

The introduction continues with a letter to parents:

> *Dear Parents,*
>
> *Being a parent is one of the most vital, and one of the most undervalued jobs in the world. We believe that you are your child's first and most important educators. Now we know how parents can help their children make a flying start at school. Here are some of the things that make a real difference, right from the start: sharing a book every day, lots of songs and rhymes, listening games, playing with shapes and belonging to the library. Libraries love baby members!*
>
> *When children start school, the support parents have given them – and continue to give them over the years – enormously influences their achievements. These folders explain how you can give that support to your child as a natural part of everyday life. They offer information and ideas, as well as showing you what a good job you are doing already. The most important part of using 'Learning Together' is the fun of talking, listening, playing, singing and sharing books together, and the confidence that it brings to parents and children.*

This project emphasises the vital role that all parents play in their children's learning from birth, ensures that parents and carers are valued for what they already do every day, and offers them information and ideas about supporting their children's development.

– LILY STARTS SCHOOL –

❛ *Today was Lily's first day at school. There was a real big fuss yesterday because Lily said Dan said you have to have a special lunch box, and she only had her old one that she and Dan used to play picnics with. She got in such a state that Mum went out and got another one, and Dad said it was ridiculous and he thought the teacher wouldn't mind what she brought her lunch in – but Lily minded. After that she was all ready, and she really wanted to go because Dan said they were going to do something special on the first day for all the new children.*

Mum and their dad were talking about Lily tonight after she was in bed. They were nearly having an argument because Mum was worried that Lily's bossy and asks lots of questions and might get into trouble and not be happy. Their dad said all mums worry too much about their children going to school, and he thought if anyone was going to do all right it was Lily. Mum asked what was so great about Lily then? And their dad suddenly got really serious and fierce and said 'I'll tell you what's great about her. She wants to know things, and she doesn't give up, and she really likes other people. She's a cracker is our Lily, and don't you forget it!' Then Mum cried and he hugged her and Lisa and me went out. ❜

Wanting to learn makes all the difference to success

In the hot seat at home

All parents want the best for their children. This is not in dispute, although what *is* sometimes disputed is the way this desire causes parents to act. Nonetheless, wanting the best for their child is a disposition that many thousands of parents have, and it represents an enormous, largely unrealised, source of energy for good. We have the key in our hands to release this energy, which is to offer relevant, appropriate and accessible information and support for parents and carers, when and where they need it.

One of the most important times to offer this information and support is when the child is just born. The birth of the baby is when the parent's disposition to do a good job in supporting a child's development is most likely to be full of optimism and joy and determination. Margaret Carr (2001) writes about dispositions as an accumulation of motivation, situation and skill in which the person with the disposition is 'ready, willing and able'. Carr's focus is on children's dispositions, but the same thinking can be used in relation to adults supporting a child's development. *Readiness* would mean being motivated or inclined to support the child; *willingness* would mean recognising when a time and situation are appropriate for support to be offered; and *ability* would mean having the knowledge, skills and understanding to support effectively. These three factors add up to possessing the disposition to support the child's development.

What does it take for parents and carers to be ready, willing and able? It is suggested that the following things help children to make a flying start: self-confidence and the disposition to learn; the ability to listen and talk and get on with other people; understanding about the uses of reading, writing, numbers and books; interest in the world. Parents and carers who are *ready* to help children with these things will be persuaded that they make a difference. Parents and carers who are *willing* to help children with these things will know how to spot the right moment; and parents and carers who are *able* to help children with these things will know what is needed, how to help, and why – and may need support. Persuasion is needed, and information, and support.

Guarding against 'dispositions erosion'

Throughout this book we have been reminded of Lily and Joe's learning dispositions. In common with the vast majority of children in their early years, Lily and Joe and their friends are voracious learners. Anyone who has lived with a baby or a toddler will recognise the boundless curiosity, the extraordinary powers of observation, the relentless questioning, the often maddening persistence, the sometimes obsessional concentration. These are the characteristics of successful learners, and it is hardly surprising that the youngest children display them in such strength when we consider what an enormous amount children of this age are learning. On the 'half empty' or 'half full' model, when it comes to learning dispositions these children are overflowing. And it is splendid that the Curriculum Guidance for the Foundation Stage acknowledges the crucial importance of positive attitudes and dispositions. Nonetheless there is something of the 'half empty' in the following words:

> *The curriculum guidance for the foundation stage should underpin all future learning by supporting, fostering, promoting and developing children's . . . positive attitudes and dispositions to learning (QCA 2000, p. 8).*

Babies and young children have all the readiness, willingness and ability to learn in the world, and it is our job as adults to support them in further developing their abilities. But as 'schooling' – or is it conformity? – gets under way, a process of erosion seems to take place which eats away at these dispositions. During the course of these first years at school, what becomes of that powerful curiosity, exploration, observation, questioning, persistence, concentration? This erosion may have as much to do with processes of social and emotional development as it does with cognitive functioning, and yet we need to ask ourselves what it is about our education systems that allows this to happen.

Instead of planning for 'supporting, fostering, promoting and developing', perhaps we should be thinking about it slightly differently. Perhaps we should be planning for recognising, valuing, protecting and using children's positive attitudes and dispositions to learn. In architectural terms, children's learning dispositions are not 'new build', they are 'conservation'.

– LISA'S LECTURE –

❟ Lisa's in trouble with her college work. It turns out that as well as keeping a sort of diary about Lily and Joe, she has to read about all the new ways that teachers are supposed to do things now with little kids. She's got three big books. One of them is from New Zealand, but the others are for here. She has to choose one part from each of the books and write something about it, and she has to think about Lily and Joe when she's doing it, it has to be about children she knows. She's worried because she has to give a sort of lecture about it to the other people at her college when she gets back next week, and she doesn't know what she's going to say. She showed me and Mum the books last night, and I said I'd help if she wants.

Then Mum said she thinks it's just what I'm interested in, and we'll help Lisa to choose the bits from the books that are really about what Lily and Joe do, so she can make the most of knowing all about them. She says these days it's much better because books like this aren't just about what children are supposed to know, they're about how children feel about themselves as well, and how they get on with other people, because that's all part of learning. Mum's right, I do think it's interesting. Maybe that's what I'll do next – go to college like Lisa. ❟

> **Self-confidence; the ability to listen and talk and get on with other people; interest in the world; understanding about the uses of reading, writing, numbers and books; the disposition to learn . . . this is how children make a flying start**

Ready, willing and able government

If *all* children are to have the opportunity to make a flying start – from all cultures, regions and socio-economic groups – there are important policy implications for government which are now beginning to be recognised. The debate about key factors in raising educational attainment is fuelled by economists as well as educators. In an influential paper on 'The Relative Economic Importance of Academic, Psychological and Behavioural Attributes Developed in Childhood', Leon Feinstein argues – with strong evidence – that 'locus of control' (in which greater self-control results in greater attentiveness in school) and self-esteem have powerful effects on labour market participation, independent of school achievement and parental background.

In a study detailing the benefits and savings generated by documented intervention programmes, Karoly, et al (1998) found that if their successes can be duplicated on a large scale, public investment in such programmes will benefit not only the children and their families but also the taxpayers who fund them. However, Karoly et al highlighted the fact that these conclusions rest primarily on smaller-scale programmes, and called for broader demonstrations and rigorous evaluations of future large-scale ones. Sure Start and Early Excellence Centres in the UK are now building on these findings, developing a wide range of new programmes with evaluations to identify their most successful elements.

Building on the evidence taken by the House of Commons Education and Employment Select Committee's review of Early Years (2000), the UK government's green paper 'Schools: Building on Success' (2001) emphasises the importance of an early years framework, describing it as

> . . . an investment in higher school standards and greater social cohesion in ten or fifteen years time. It is a crucial step towards breaking the cycle of deprivation . . . Children's experiences in the earliest years of their life are critical to their subsequent development. They have a significant impact on their future performance at school and the extent to which they are able to take advantage of opportunities later in life.

The progress of Sure Start programmes and Centres of Excellence, and the important work of the Pen Green Centre, Coram Family and many many others, will ensure the development of a range of ways of supporting children's ability to learn, and the issues involved. But support for *all* children will take more than this. There is a strong case to be made for a universal service to support children's development from birth to school. And yet, there is already in existence a universal service for the youngest children – that provided by their parents and carers. In reality it is universal support for parents and carers that is needed, starting from the birth of the child, sensitively offered and encompassing the whole range of children's emotional, social and cognitive development in addition to health.

A vision for the future

The pace of change around us is accelerating. Traditional authorities are undermined in a variety of ways: by demographic changes, by social and family modifications, by the global market place, by new technology, by challenges to security.

All these factors will have a profound effect on our lives. We seem to have lost our way in terms of values and family life. The need to find a new sense of direction highlights the urgency of many of the issues raised in this book.

In an article entitled 'Tilting the Balance', Tom Leimdorfer (1993) suggested ways of working towards a more hopeful vision of the future. He proposed five basic ingredients as priorities in our educational climate: an affirming climate (positive self-images, valuing ourselves and others), a listening climate, a co-operative climate, a problem-solving climate and a human rights climate. Here, indeed, is a vision for the future, the essence of which has been foreshadowed many times in the past. Joan Riviere (1927, reprinted 1955) was the analyst of both Winnicott and Bowlby; echoing John Donne, she wrote:

> There is no such thing as a single human being, pure and simple, unmixed with other human beings. Each personality is a world in himself, a company of many. That self . . . is a composite structure . . . formed out of countless never-ending influences and exchanges between ourselves and others. These other persons are in fact therefore part of ourselves . . . we are members of one another.

Early childhood is '. . . a period of momentous significance for all people growing up in [our] culture – by the time this period is over, children will have formed conceptions of themselves as social beings, as thinkers, and as language users, and they will have reached certain important decisions about their own abilities and their own worth' (Donaldson et al, 1983).

It should be acknowledged that some concerns now exist as to the value of early high self-esteem, raising the possibility that high self-esteem might encourage children to be self-centred and selfish. Certainly it is recognised that how children learn to see themselves, right from the start, makes a profound impact on their self-esteem throughout life. But these concerns relate, quite rightly, to self-esteem that is based on constant, automatic and undiscriminating praise.

This book highlights every child's need for acceptance, while making the case for adults' careful observation of children, and for setting limits. Genuine recognition of children's *real* efforts and achievements has been argued here to be the basis of their realistic self-esteem and the inner confidence that underpins effective learning. Children who have learned from their important adults to value their own genuine efforts and achievements are more likely to believe they *can* learn, and so to learn successfully . . . not only as they start school, but throughout school and for the rest of their lives.

Epilogue

Tomorrow I'm going away to college. They gave me some money to get things, and I've done the washing and got my stuff together, so I'm ready. Lisa says she'll help me settle in.

I'm going to miss everyone, especially Lily and Joe. Lily says she's coming with me. She hasn't figured out that you can't be in two places at once, so if she comes with me she won't have Mum and her dad; she thinks she can be with me and be at home as well.

She's right, though, as usual. She's coming with me in my head. I'll never forget them – Mum and dad and Lily and Joe.

POSTSCRIPT TO PART 6: READY, WILLING AND ABLE
Living or working with young children?
Questions to think about . . .

> **Talking, listening, playing and singing together, and sharing books every day . . . from birth all children need opportunities to do these things, with people they love and admire who recognise, value and encourage their efforts and achievements**

1. What do babies and young children really mind about?

> ***Wanting* to learn makes all the difference to success**

2. Why is it that some children seem to want to learn and some don't? What is the basis of a life-long disposition to learn?

> **Self-confidence; the ability to listen and talk and get on with other people; interest in the world; understanding about the uses of reading, writing, numbers and books; the disposition to learn . . . this is how children make a flying start**

3. What is needed – in families, in communities, and in national policy – so that all children can be offered the opportunities they need for their well-being and development?

RECOMMENDED FURTHER READING

For sharing with children . . .

Briggs, R. (1970), *Jim and the Beanstalk*, **London, Puffin Books**
Jim has all the positive learning dispositions – he's exploratory, questioning, a listener, and a persistent problem solver. Undoubtedly ready, willing and able to help the giant, Jim does however lack an element of foresight, and only just escapes being fried and served up on toast for breakfast. But he very properly ends up with his just reward, to his mother's relief. Children love the suspense, and this book is full of humour for adults too.

For a good read . . .

Carr, M. (2001), *Assessment in Early Childhood Settings: Learning Stories*, **London, Paul Chapman Publishing**
Abandoning the general notion of a body of requisite knowledge and skills at school entry, Margaret Carr suggests that the ultimate goals of early education should have much more to do with learning dispositions such as resilience, confidence and collaboration. Her important book is a timely reminder of the complexities and ambitions of young children and their learning, and the skillful and sensitive role of adults in effectively supporting and assessing them.

For reference . . .

QCA (2000), *Curriculum Guidance for the Foundation Stage*, **London, Qualifications and Curriculum Authority**
Inevitably the Curriculum Guidance will make an enormous impact on the development of the learning and teaching of young children in the twenty-first century. Delineating six areas of learning with progression from age three to the end of the foundation stage, it includes stepping stones for helping practitioners to plan; examples of what children do, to help practitioners assess; and what the practitioner needs to do, to help practitioners to teach. This is a profoundly influential document that will affect all our children.

Key statements

Say 'yes' as often as you can
and when you say 'no', mean it

PART 1 BABIES FIRST

Babies and young children need to feel accepted by
their important people

How babies and young children learn to see
themselves is significantly affected by their growing
knowledge of how to be acceptable to us

Babies and young children generally behave according
to how they see themselves

PART 2   FUNDAMENTAL FEELINGS

As well as feeling love and pleasure, it is normal for people to feel pain, anxiety and anger

Denied pain, anxiety and anger all undermine positive self-concept – these feelings are hard to acknowledge and manage unless they are recognised by others as normal and acceptable

Babies and young children can manage pain, anxiety and anger more easily if they know that other people accept and sympathise with how they feel

PART 3   OTHER PEOPLE

'Unreasonable' behaviour is almost always reasonable from the point of view of the baby or young child doing it

It is possible to accept and sympathise with babies' and young children's pain, anxiety and anger without having to accept 'unreasonable' behaviour generated by those feelings

Children learn to be responsible by taking responsibility

PART 4   LINKING WITH LEARNING

> **Learning involves struggle and adjustment. Too much struggle is overwhelming. Too little struggle means no adjustment**

> **Some learning skills come naturally; these include exploring,questioning, experimenting and learning from mistakes**

> **In order to be 'socially acceptable', children often learn to behave in ways that inhibit learning**

PART 5   REAL SELF-ESTEEM

> **Children are encouraged to learn when someone knows what they especially want to do and can nearly manage, and helps them to manage it successfully**

> **Recognising and supporting the development of children's patterns of learning, or schemas, leads to high self-esteem**

> **Children learn well with a combination of appropriately high expectations and appropriately high self-esteem**

PART 6   READY, WILLING AND ABLE

Talking, listening, playing and singing together, and sharing books every day . . . from birth all children need opportunities to do these things, with people they love and admire who recognise, value and encourage their efforts and achievements

Wanting to learn makes all the difference to success

Self-confidence; the ability to listen and talk and get on with other people; interest in the world; understanding about the uses of reading, writing, numbers and books; the disposition to learn . . . this is how children make a flying start

Bibliography

Abbott, L. and Pugh, C. (1998), *Training to Work in the Early Years*, Buckingham, Open University Press

Abbott, L. and Moylett, H. (1999), *Early Education Transformed*, London, Falmer Press

Abbott, L. and Nutbrown, C. (2001), *Experiencing Reggio Emilia*, Buckingham, Open University Press

Athey, C. (1990), *Extending Thought in Young Children*, London, Paul Chapman Publishing

BBC/National Children's Bureau (1999), *Tuning into Children*, London, BBC Education Production

Bagley, C., Verma, G., Mallick, M. and Young, L. (1979), *Personality, Self-esteem and Prejudice*, London, Saxon House

Ball, C. (1994), *Start Right: The Importance of Early Learning*, London, RSA

Bannister, D. and Fransella, F. (1986), *Inquiring Man: The Psychology of Personal Constructs*, London, Croom Helm

Barnes, P. (1995), *Personal, Social and Emotional Development of Children*, Oxford, Basil Blackwell

Bartholomew, L. and Bruce, T. (1993), *Getting to Know You*, London, Hodder and Stoughton

Becker, E. (1971), *The Birth and Death of Meaning*, London, Penguin Books

Bettelheim, B. (1987), *A Good Enough Parent*, London, Thames and Hudson

Bick, E. (1963), 'Notes on Infant Observation in Psychoanalytic Training' in M. Harris Williams (ed.), *Collected Papers of Martha Harris and Esther Bick*, Strath Tay, The Clunie Press

Bion, W.R. (1962), *Learning From Experience*, London, Heinemann

Black, D. (1991), 'The Red Judge' in *Collected Poems: 1964–87*, Edinburgh, Polygon

Blakemore, S.J. (2000), *Early Years Learning*, London, Parliamentary Office of Science and Technology

Blenkin, G. and Kelly, A. (1992), *Assessment in Early Childhood Education*, London, Paul Chapman Publishing

Bower, T. (1977), *A Primer of Infant Development*, San Francisco, Freeman

Bowlby, J. (1969), *Attachment*, London, Penguin Books

Bowlby, J. (1973), *Separation*, London, Penguin Books

Bowlby, J. (1980), *Loss*, London, Penguin Books

Brazelton, T. (1992), *Touch points*, London, Viking

Brice Heath, S. (1983), *Ways With Words*, Cambridge, Cambridge University Press

Briggs, R. (1970), *Jim and the Beanstalk*, London, Puffin Books

Briggs, R. (1978), *The Snowman*, London, Hamish Hamilton

Brooks, G., Gorman, T., Harman, J., Hutchinson, D. and Wilkin, A., (1996) *Family Literacy Works*, London, The Basic Skills Agency

Brown, B. (1998), *Unlearning Discrimination in the Early Years*, Stoke on Trent, Trentham Books Ltd

Bruce, T. (1987), *Early Childhood Education*, London, Hodder and Stoughton

Bruce, T. (1991), *Time To Play in Early Childhood Education*, London, Hodder and Stoughton

Bruce, T. (1996), *Helping Young Children to Play*, London, Hodder and Stoughton

Bruce,T., and Meggitt, C. (1999), *Child Care and Education* (Second Edition), London, Hodder and Stoughton

Bruce, T. (2001), *Learning Through Play – Babies, Toddlers, and the Foundation Years*, London, Hodder and Stoughton

Bruner, J. (1962), *On Knowing*, Cambridge, Massachusetts, Belknap Press

Bruner, J. (1971), *The Relevance of Education*, London, Allen and Unwin

Bruner, J. and Haste, H. (1987), *Making Sense*, London, Routledge

Buchanan, A. and Hudson, B.L. (1998), *Parenting, Schooling and Children's Behaviour*, Aldershot, Ashgate Publishing Ltd

Burningham, J. (1973) *Mr Gumpy's Outing*, London, Puffin Books

Canfield, J. and Wells, H. (1976), *100 Ways to Enhance Self-Concept in the Classroom*, New Jersey, Prentice Hall

Carr, M. (2001), *Assessment in Early Childhood Settings: Learning Stories*, London, Paul Chapman Publishing

Chukovsky, K. (1966), *From Two to Five*, California, University of California Press

Claxton, G. (1984), *Live and Learn*, London, Harper and Row

Claxton, G. (1997), *Hare Brain, Tortoise Mind – Why Intelligence Increases when you Think Less*, London, Fourth Estate

Crocker, A.C. and Cheeseman, R.G. (1988), 'Infant teachers have a major impact on children's self-awareness' in *Children & Society*, 2, 3–8

Curry, N. and Johnson, C. (1990), *Beyond Self-Esteem: Developing a Genuine Sense of Human Value*, Washington DC, NAEYC

Curtis, A. (1992), 'How Competent Are Our Young Children?' in *Early Education*, 5, 9–10

David, T. (1990), *Under five – under-educated?*, Buckingham, Open University Press

David, T., Raban, B., Ure, C., Goouch, K., Jago, M. and Barriere, I. (2000), *Making Sense of Early Literacy*, Stoke on Trent, Trentham Books Ltd

Desforges, C. (1989), 'Understanding Learning for Teaching' in *Westminster Studies in Education*, 12, 2, 17–29

D.E.S. (1989), *The Education of Children Under Five*, London, HMSO

D.E.S. (1990), *Starting With Quality: The Report of Enquiry into the Quality of the Educational Experience Offered to Three- and Four-Year-Olds*, London, HMSO

Docking, J. (1980), *Control and Discipline*, London, Harper and Row

Donaldson, M. (1978), *Children's Minds*, London, Fontana Press

Donaldson, M., Grieve, R. and Pratt, C. (1983), *Early Childhood Development and Education: Readings in Psychology*, Oxford, Basil Blackwell

Donaldson, M. and Elliot, T. (1990), 'Children's Explanations' in R. Grieve and M. Hugh (eds), *Understanding Children*, Oxford, Blackwell

Dowling, M. (2000), *Young Children's Personal, Social and Emotional Development*, London, Paul Chapman Publishing

Driver, R. (1983), *The Pupil as Scientist*, Oxford, Oxford University Press

Drummond, M.J. (1993), *Assessing Children's Learning*, London, David Fulton

Drummond, M.J. (1999), *Comparisons in Early Years Education: History, Fact and Fiction*, University of Warwick, Centre for Research in Elementary and Primary Education

Dunn, J. (1984), *Sisters and Brothers*, London, Fontana

Dunn, J. (1988), *The Beginnings of Social Understanding*, Oxford, Blackwell

Dunn, J. (1993), *Young Children's Close Relationships*, London, Sage Publications

Early Childhood Education Forum (1998), *Quality in Diversity in Early Learning*, London, National Children's Bureau

Edelman, G. (1992), *Bright Air, Brilliant Fire: On the Matter of the Mind*, London, The Penguin Press

English, H.B. and English, A.C. (1958), *A Comprehensive Dictionary of Psychological and Psychoanalytical Terms*, London, Longman

Erikson, E. (1950), *Childhood and Society*, London, Paladin

Feinstein, L. (2000), *The Relative Importance of Academic, Psychological and Behavioural Attributes Developed in Childhood*, London, Centre for Economic Performance

Fisher, J. (1996), *Starting from the Child*, Buckingham, Open University Press

Fisher, J. (ed), (2002), *The Foundations of Learning*, Buckingham, Open University Press

Fountain, S. (1990), *Learning Together*, Cheltenham, Stanley Thornes

Freud, S. (1977), *Case Histories* 1, London, Penguin Books

Galloway, F. (1987), 'PSE Teaching Pack' in Appendix 3 *Personal and Social Education in the Primary School*, University of York, Diploma in Applied Educational Studies

Gardner, H. (1993), *Frames of Mind: The Theory of Multiple Intelligence*, New York, Basic Books

Gardner, H. (1993), 'Complementary Perspectives on Reggio Emilia', in Edwards, C., Gandini, L., Forman, G., *The Hundred Languages of Children – The Reggio Emilia Approach to Early Childhood Education*, New Jersey, Ablex

Goldschmied, E. and Jackson, S. (1994), *People Under Three*, London, Routledge

Gopnik, A., Meltzoff, A. and Kuhl, P. (1999), *How Babies Think*, London, Weidenfeld and Nicolson

Gore, A. (1992), *Earth In The Balance*, London, Earthscan

Grieve, R. and Hughes, M. (1990), *Understanding Children*, Oxford, Blackwell

Gura, P. (ed.) (1992), *Exploring Learning: Young Children and Blockplay*, London, Paul Chapman Publishing

Hannon, P. (1995), *Literacy, Home and School*, London, Falmer Press

Harris, M. (1987), 'Some Notes on Maternal Containment', in M. Harris Williams (ed.), *Collected Papers of Martha Harris and Esther Bick*, Strath Tay, The Clunie Press

Harris, P.L. (1989), *Children And Emotion – the Development of Psychological Understanding*, Oxford, Basil Blackwell

Herbert, M. (1996) *Feuding and Fighting: A Guide to the Management of Aggression and Quarrelling in Children*, London, The British Psychological Society

Herbert, M. (1996) *Setting Limits: Promoting Positive Parenting*, London, The British Psychological Society

Hitz, R. and Driscoll, A. (1988), 'New Insights Into Praise: Implications for Early Childhood Teachers' in *Young Children*, July

Holditch, L. (1992), *Understanding Your Five-Year-Old*, London, Rosendale Press

Holmes, J. (1993), *John Bowlby and Attachment Theory*, London, Routledge

Holt, J. (1983), *How Children Learn*, London, Penguin Books

Honess, T. and Yardley, K. (1987), *Self and Identity: Perspectives across the Lifespan*, London, Routledge and Kegan Paul

House of Commons Education and Employment Committee (2000), *First Report: Early Years*, London, The Stationery Office

Hudson, L. (1975), *Human Beings*, London, Jonathan Cape

Hurst, V. (1991), *Planning for Early Learning*, London, Paul Chapman Publishing

Isaacs, S. (1954), *The Educational Value of the Nursery School*, London, The British Association for Early Childhood Education

Jowett, S. and Sylva, K. (1986), 'Does Kind of Pre-School Matter?' in *Educational Research*, 28, 1, 21–31

Karoly, L.A., Greenwood, P.W., Everingham, S.S, Hoube, J., Kiburn, M.R. Rydell, C.P., Sanders, M. and Chiesa, J. (1998), *Investing in our Children: What we Know and Don't Know about the Costs and Benefits of Early Childhood Interventions*, Washington, RAND

Katz, L.G. (1993), Dispositions: Definitions and Implications for Early Childhood Practices Perspectives from ERIC/ECCE: a monograph series. Urbana, Illinois: ERIC Clearinghouse on ECCE

Katz, L.G. (1995), *Talks with Teachers of Young Children*, New Jersey, Ablex Publishing Corporation

Kelly, G.A. (1955), *The Psychology of Personal Constructs*, New York, Norton

Kelly, G.A. (1970), 'A brief introduction to personal construct theory' in D. Bannister (ed.), *Perspectives in Personal Construct Theory*, Academic Press

Klein, M. (1975a), *Love, Guilt and Reparation*, London, Virago

Klein, M. (1975b), *Envy and Gratitude*, London, Virago

Konner, M. (1991), *Childhood*, London, Little, Brown and Company

Laevers, F. (2000), 'Forward to Basics! Deep-Level Learning and the Experiantial Approach', in *Early Years* 20, 2, 20–9

Lally, M. (1991), *The Nursery Teacher in Action*, London, Paul Chapman Publishing

Lawrence, D. (1987), *Enhancing Self-Esteem in the Classroom*, London, Paul Chapman Publishing

Leach, P. (1997), *Your Baby and Child – New Version for a New Generation*, London, Penguin

Lee, V. & Das Gupta, P. (1995) *Children's Cognitive and Language Development*, Buckingham, Open University Press

Leimdorfer, T. (1993), 'Tilting the Balance' in *The Friend*, 27th August

Leslie, A. (1987), 'Pretence and Representation: The Origins of "Theory of Mind" in *Psychological Review*, 94, 4, 412–26

Light, P. (1979), *The Development of Social Sensitivity*, Cambridge, Cambridge University Press

Lindon, J. (2000), *Helping Babies and Toddlers Learn*, London, National Early Years Network

Logan, R. (1987), 'Historical Change in Prevailing Sense of Self' in K. Yardley and T. Honess (eds), *Self and Identity: Psychological Perspectives*, Chichester, John Wiley

MacFarlane, J.A. (1977), *The Psychology of Childbirth*, Oxford, Oxford University Press

Magee, B. (1973), *Popper*, London, Fontana

Makins, V. (1997), *Not Just a Nursery Rhyme*, London, National Children's Bureau

Malaguzzi, L. (1987), *The Hundred Languages of Children: Narrative of the Possible*, Catalogue of the 'Hundred Languages of Children' exhibition, Reggio Emilia, Comune di Reggio Emilia

Malaguzzi, L. (1997) in Penn, H., *Comparing Nurseries: Staff and Children in Italy, Spain and the UK*, London, Paul Chapman Publishing

Markus, H. and Nurius, P. (1987), 'Possible selves: The Interface between Motivation and the Self-concept', in K. Yardley and T. Honess (eds), *Self and Identity*, Chichester, John Wiley

Marshall, H. (1989), 'The Development of Self-Concept' in *Young Children*, July

Maslow, A. (1968), *Toward a Psychology of Being*, New York, Van Nostrand Reinhold

Matthews, J. (1987), 'The Young Child's Early Representation and Drawing' in G. Blenkin and A. Kelly (eds), *Early Childhood Education: a Development Curriculum*, London, Paul Chapman Publishing

Matthews, J. (1994), *Helping Children to Draw and Paint: Visual Representation*, London, Hodder and Stoughton

Mead, G. (1934), *Mind, Self and Society*, Chicago, University of Chicago Press

Meade, A. (2000), *The Brain Debate*, Wellington, Fullbright Lecture

Medawar, P. (1981), *Pluto's Republic*, Oxford, Oxford University Press

Miedzian, M. (1992), *Boys Will Be Boys*, London, Virago

Miller, A. (1979), *The Drama of Being a Child*, London, Virago

Miller, L. (1992a), *Understanding Your Baby*, London, Rosendale Press

Miller, L. (1992b), *Understanding Your Four-Year-Old*, London, Rosendale Press

Moyles, J. (ed.) (1994), *The Excellence of Play*, Buckingham, Open University Press

Nash, R. (1976), *Teacher Expectations and Pupil Learning*, London, Routledge and Kegan Paul

National Commission on Education (1993), *Learning to Succeed*, London, Heinemann

New Zealand Ministry of Education (1996), Te Whariki, *Early Childhood Curriculum*, Wellington, Learning Media

Nutbrown, C. (1994), *Threads of Thinking*, London, Paul Chapman Publishing

Paley, V. (1992), *You Can't Say You Can't Play*, Cambridge, Massachusetts, Harvard University Press

Pascal, C. (1990), *Under-Fives in the Infant Classroom*, Stoke-on-Trent, Trentham Books

Pascal, C. and Bertram, T. (1997), *Effective Early Learning: Case Studies in Improvement*, London, Hodder and Stoughton

Perez-Sanchez, M. (1990), *Baby Observation: Emotional Relationships During the First Year of Life*, Strath Tay, Clunie Press

Piaget, J. (1951), *Play, Dreams and Imitation in Childhood*, London, Routledge and Kegan Paul

Piaget, J. (1953), *The Origin of Intelligence in the Child*, London, Routledge and Kegan Paul

Pines, M. (1987), 'Mirroring and Child Development' in T. Honess and K. Yardley (eds), *Self and Identity*, London, Routledge and Kegan Paul

Pollard, A. and Tann, S. (1987), *Reflective Teaching in the Primary School*, London, Cassell Education

QCA (2000), *Curriculum Guidance for the Foundation Stage*, London, Qualifications and Curriculum Authority

Reid, S. (1992), *Understanding Your Two-Year-Old*, London, Rosendale Press

Riviere, J. (1955), 'The unconscious phantasy of an inner world reflected in examples from literature' in M. Klein, P. Heimann and R. Money-Kyrle (eds), *New Directions in Psychoanalysis*, London, Hogarth

Roberts, R. (1993), *Self-Concept and Learning Skills at Four Years Old*, unpublished MA dissertation, Oxford Brookes University

Roberts, R. (ed.), *A Nursery Education Curriculum for the Early Years*, Oxford, National Primary Centre

Roberts, R. (ed.) (2000), *The Learning Together Series*, Oxford, PEEP

Roberts, R. (ed.) (2000), *PEEP Voices – a Five-Year Diary*, Oxford, PEEP

Roberts, R. (ed.) (2001), *Making the Most of PEEP*, Oxford, PEEP

Rogers, C. (1961), *On Becoming a Person*, London, Constable

Rycroft, C. (1968), *A Critical Dictionary of Psychoanalysis*, London, Penguin Books

Salmon, W. (1988), *Psychology for Teachers*, London, Hutchinson

Sammons, P. et al (1999), *Technical Paper 2: Characteristics of the EPPE Project Sample at Entry to the Study*, London, Institute of Education University of London

Sheridan, M. (1991), 'Increasing Self-Esteem and Competency in Children' in *International Journal of Early Childhood*, 23, 1, 28–35

Shore, R. (1997), *Rethinking the Brain – New Insights into Early Development*, New York, Families and Work Institute

Singer, D. and Singer, J. (1990), *The House of Make-Believe*, Cambridge, Massachusetts, Harvard University Press

Siraj-Blatchford, I. and Siraj-Blatchford, J. (1995) *Educating the Whole Child: Cross-Curricular Skills, Themes and Dimensions*, Buckingham, Open University Press

Siraj-Blatchford, I. (ed) (1998), *A Curriculum Development Handbook for Early Childhood Educators*, Stoke on Trent, Trentham Books Ltd

Skemp, R. (1979), *Intelligence, Learning and Action*, Chichester, John Wiley

Smith, F. (1978), *Reading*, Cambridge, Cambridge University Press

Steiner, D. (1992), *Understanding Your One-Year-Old*, London, Rosendale Press

Storr, A. (1960), *The Integrity of the Personality*, London, Penguin Books

Stott, D., Green, L. and Francis, J. (1988), *The Guide to the Child's Learning Skills*, Stafford, NARE Publications

Sure Start Unit (2000), *Providing Good Quality Childcare and Early Learning Experience through Sure Start*, Nottingham, DfEE Publications

Sure Start Unit (2000), *Sure Start – Making a Difference for Children and Families*, Nottingham, DfEE Publications

Sylva, K. (1994), 'The Impact of Early Learning on Children's Later Development' in C. Ball (ed.), *Start Right: The Importance of Early Learning*, London, RSA

Tizard, B. and Hughes, M. (1984), *Young Children Learning*, London, Fontana

Trowell, J. (1992), *Understanding Your Three-Year-Old*, London, Rosendale Press

Vygotsky, L. (1978), *Mind in Society*, Cambridge, Massachusetts, Harvard University Press

Waddell, M. & Firth, B. (1999) *Well Done, Little Bear*, London, Walker Books

Waddell, M. & Benson, P. (1992), *Owl Babies*, London, Walker Books

Weinberger, J. (1996), *Literacy Goes to School: The Parents' Role in Young Children's Literacy Learning*, London, Paul Chapman Publishing

Waldegrave, W. (1991), *The Health of the Nation*, London, HMSO

Wells, G. (1986), *The Meaning Makers*, London, Hodder and Stoughton

Whalley, M. (1994), *Learning To Be Strong*, London, Hodder and Stoughton

Whalley, M. (1997), *Working with Parents as Partners in Education and Care*, London, Hodder and Stoughton

Whalley, M. (2000), *Involving Parents in their Children's Learning*, London, Paul Chapman Publishing

Winkley, L. (1991), 'Children's Emotional Needs: A Child Psychiatrist's View' *in Special Issue in Primary Education*, 1, 8–11

Winnicott, D.W. (1964), *The Child, the Family and the Outside World*, London, Penguin Books

Winnicott, D.W. (1971), 'Mirror-role of mother and family in child development' in *Playing and Reality*, London, Tavistock Publications

Winnicott, D.W. (1986), *Home Is Where We Start From*, London, Penguin Books

Wishinsky, F. & Thompson, C. (1998), *OONGA BOONGA Big Brother's Magic Words*, London, Picture Corgi

Wolfendale, S. and Bryans, T. (1989), *Managing Behaviour*, Stafford, NARE Publications

Wolff, R.P. (ed.) (1968), *Kant: A Collection of Critical Essays*, London, Macmillan

Wylie, C. (1996) *Five Years Old and Competent*, Wellington, New Zealand Council for Educational Research

Wylie, C. (1998) *Six Years Old and Competent*, Wellington, New Zealand Council for Educational Research

Yardley, K. and Honess, T. (1987), *Self and Identity: Psychological Perspectives*, Chichester, John Wiley

Ziman, E. (1950), *Jealousy in Children*, London, Gollancz

Index